"What could be more valuable to us than family? But what could be more divisive and troubling than the way the term 'family values' has been used as a weapon in today's culture wars? I'm so glad that Erin Wathen has given us a fresh take on family values in her beautifully written, very readable new book, *More than Words*. Mom, blogger, and pastor, Erin is a writer worth following, starting with *More than Words*."

—Brian D. McLaren,
author of *The Great Spiritual Migration*

"Erin Wathen is a welcome voice of love, justice, and mercy for those of us who cringe at how the term 'family values' has been misused in our political landscape. *More than Words* is full of practical wisdom, guiding us in those unique and beautiful relationships, with all their abundance."

—Carol Howard Merritt,
author of *Healing Spiritual Wounds*

"Family values have long been at the cherished center of the Christian heart, but somewhere along the way the entire concept of family values became synonymous with bigotry, hate, and exclusion. In *More than Words*, Erin Wathen beautifully reclaims what this term was originally intended to be—a manifesto that leads one to a life of justice, love, and beauty."

—Benjamin L. Corey, author of
Undiluted: Rediscovering the Radical Message of Jesus

"Increasingly, it seems, we live in a world more focused on differences and divisions than on points of commonality. Wathen takes that unfortunate reality head-on, presenting us with values we can all get onboard with and, in doing so, provides a common ground around which to grow our families and communities in even healthier and more nurturing ways. Her book is personal, engaging, honest, real, and biblically grounded. It's difficult to imagine any Christian who wouldn't find value, growth, and enjoyment in Wathen's perspective."

—Mark Sandlin, cofounder of The Christian Left,
blogger for *Huffington Post* and Patheos,
and ordained minister in the PC(USA)

More than Words

More than Words

10 Values for the Modern Family

Erin Wathen

WESTMINSTER
JOHN KNOX PRESS
LOUISVILLE · KENTUCKY

First edition
Published by Westminster John Knox Press
Louisville, Kentucky

17 18 19 20 21 22 23 24 25 26—10 9 8 7 6 5 4 3 2 1

Book design by Drew Stevens
Cover design by Mary Ann Smith
Cover illustration: Mary Ann Smith

Library of Congress Cataloging-in-Publication Data

Names: Wathen, Erin, author.
Title: More than words : 10 values for the modern family / Erin Wathen.
Description: Louisville, KY : Westminster John Knox Press, 2017.
Identifiers: LCCN 2016052020 (print) | LCCN 2017004072 (ebook) | ISBN 9780664262945 (pbk. : alk. paper) | ISBN 9781611648041 (ebk.)
Subjects: LCSH: Families--Religious life. | Families--Religious aspects--Christianity. | Families. | Conduct of life. | Values.
Classification: LCC BV4526.3 .W36 2017 (print) | LCC BV4526.3 (ebook) | DDC 248.4--dc23
LC record available at https://lccn.loc.gov/2016052020

Most Westminster John Knox Press books are available at special quantity discounts when purchased in bulk by corporations, organizations, and special-interest groups. For more information, please e-mail SpecialSales@wjkbooks.com.

For Jeremy, Harper, and Silas.
Who make me crazy, and make my house a home.

Contents

Acknowledgments

Gratitude is a family value, so I need to express mine for the people and places that make up our village. This book is a collective of friends and neighbors; my own family, near and far; and the congregations that have "raised" me.

Many thanks to Annie Kratzsch, for letting me share some of her writing within my own; to Courtney Smith and Stephanie Whisner for creating KindCraft and letting me share their story; to the wonderful community of our elementary school, which daily reinforces these values in the classroom and beyond; to the extended community of Patheos readers, who have shaped my voice and contributed to this broader conversation for years; to Foothills Christian Church in Phoenix, for the many ways they made a pastor of me; and to the folks at Saint Andrew Christian Church, who live these values with such faithfulness, and who support their pastor's writing habit in such generous fashion.

Thanks to Jessica Miller Kelley, WJK editor extraordinaire— who not only thought I could maybe write a book, but made a living, breathing thing of my rambling, winding words.

Because I am a gypsy, I tend to run with other wandering souls. And so my extended network of family and close friends reaches from coast to coast—though it is firmly anchored in the hills of Kentucky. For all of you who let me be who I am— and love me anyway—I am grateful beyond telling. I hope that you see yourselves in these pages, in the many ways that I mirror the best of you to the world around me. Now that I am done with this book, I promise to visit more.

Introduction

I was drinking a beer. That was her first clue that I wasn't a "real Christian." When she asked me what I did and I mentioned that I was a pastor, I'm guessing that sealed the deal.

So when she asked me to tell her about my church, I could have quoted our denomination's identity statement, keeping it light and generic. Or I could have told her about youth group and women's ministries and mission work in El Salvador. But I could tell by her upbeat yet mildly confrontational air that I was already batting zero—drinking a beer AND being a lady minister—so I went down the rabbit hole.

"Well," I said, "we really emphasize community and service. We are concerned about the environment, and poverty, and other global justice issues. We have local and global mission projects that are focused on sustainability and empowerment. And, we are welcoming and inclusive of LGBT people."

More on that trip down the rabbit hole later, and why I talk to strangers in places like Whole Foods, and the Whole Foods bar. But for now, I'll just say that the whole scene ended in her shaming me for my faulty and dangerous interpretation of

Scripture with a mini-sermon about Jesus, marriage, and "family values"—not necessarily in that order.

This was not an isolated incident. Any time someone in my vicinity starts talking about standing for "family values," the clear implication is that *I don't*. Or that my church doesn't.

But isn't nonviolence a value? Isn't hospitality? Isn't diversity? Those are family values. At least, they are in my family. Why do we find ourselves on the outside of the commonly accepted parameters of "values-based" living?

In the current political climate, "family values" has become code language covering all manner of sins from misogyny to homophobia to a sick romance with guns. Tack on a not-so-subtle xenophobia—fear or hatred of anything that is not distinctly American and Christian—and it all adds up to a language of rigidity, strict gender norms, and biblically condoned judgment and shame.

As a result, many people outside of that traditional base now associate those words, "family values," with exclusion, bigotry, and a worldview that is distinctly homophobic and misogynistic, and subtly violent.

In response to this cultural trend, progressive churches have pulled back from talking about "family" at all. We don't want to exclude those whose homes don't fit in the box of a traditional, nuclear family, and we certainly don't want to be associated with "*those* Christians." The ones who say that God called all women to be homemakers, that the gays are going to burn in hell, and that we should all homeschool our children to keep them away from the scary science books.

We don't want to get sucked down that particular rabbit hole. But does that mean we have to abandon this conversation entirely?

Because values *do* have an important role in our lives. They inform our decisions and shape our relationships—and we build communities of faith around shared *values*. So maybe there is a way to reclaim those values, and a language for exploring them, as something life-giving—and ultimately, deeply important to the work of living faith together.

But we need an entirely new lexicon. One that avoids the judgment and the rigid imposition of outdated cultural norms and instead gives light and life to the family that *is* and not to the one that someone else says should be. We need a language that reflects the inclusion, love, and hope for a better world that we know to be at the heart of the gospel, while at the same time deepening our connections to family, neighbor, and faith community.

Words matter, and the right words can help shape our identity and intentions. But even with the right language in place, it is easy to reduce a set of values to a collection of bumper-sticker-worthy sound bites. Beyond the new vocabulary, what today's families need are practices—ways to actively live into those values both at home and in community.

Nobody has all the answers, and there is no way to prescribe a set of behaviors that will work for every person or family unit. In fact, that is exactly what fundamentalists have done for decades, and that approach has often done a great deal of harm to families and faith communities. I want to help families talk creatively about what matters to *them*; to order their time, their money, and their intentions around that which will give them life, and make the world a better place; and to connect in meaningful, everyday ways that will sustain them through difficult seasons.

This book is not meant to draw a line in the sand between progressive and more conservative Christians, perpetuating the divisiveness already fracturing our communities and churches. On the contrary, this conversation could provide some common ground as we move forward together. Too often, people on the more progressive end of the theological and social spectrum rush to point out what is wrong with another system of belief, without providing an alternative. In this book, we'll explore the language of a better way; a more life-giving way; a way that leaves room for creativity, for questions, for imperfection, and for a much broader view of what it means to be "family."

I say this acknowledging that we all want the same things— you, me, the woman at the Whole Foods bar—we all want healthy families, meaningful connections, strong communities, and to see the good news of radical love and mercy embodied in our time and place.

What follows is a journey toward acting out that sacred desire in our own homes, neighborhoods, and churches. It is a series of stories, practices, and discussion questions to use with the people we love: whether that "family" expression looks like a Norman Rockwell Christmas card, the Griswold Family Vacation, or the cast of *Rent*. It is a choose-your-own-adventure guide, because there is no one way to be family.

And isn't that good news?

1
Compassion: Love in Action

It's 8 a.m. Prime time in the elementary school drop-off line. In other words: the first moment of my day to truly test the limits of my love for humankind.

I can wake up feeling refreshed and well rested. I can start my day with a peaceful moment of prayer on the back deck, coffee in hand and the whole day shimmering lovely ahead of me. I can laugh through breakfast with my children, kiss my spouse good-bye, and head out the door in comfortable shoes with a fully charged phone. I am like Snow White, complete with birds singing around my head. All is right with the world.

But then, there's the car line. There's a person in a giant SUV making an *illegal left turn* into the school to cut in line— because clearly rules don't apply to them and they are in a hurry and they are *important*—and I am suddenly filled with rage. All that deep yoga breathing and morning prayer goes out the window, and I become the worst caricature of suburban life. "*They only send home a weekly paper note and a daily email, reminding you to go to the back of the line!*" I shout to no one. "*It's completely understandable that you don't know any better!*"

At least my windows are tinted. So I've got that going for me.

Love is the first family value. Most people, from any background or faith framework, would claim it as a critical core of belief, whether that means love of family, love for community and neighbor, or love for creation. The trouble is . . . love can become a cultural abstraction, impossibly vague and intangible. Love can be easily reduced to a word on a page or a greeting card sentiment, hijacked by the entertainment industry for the purposes of another formulaic rom-com, or applied haphazardly to the most surface-level things in our lives. I love coffee. And wine. And *Harry Potter*. And vacation. I *really* love vacation. And also wine. Especially after a week of navigating the drop-off line. Mercy.

We "love" lots of things that we can name, touch, taste, and see. And yet, the same expression of "love" gets applied, uniformly, to our most meaningful connections. Clearly, my love for, say, the perfect BLT is not the same as my love for my children. Or the love that a church family expresses in caring community.

How can we root a values system in love when the means of expression are so nebulous? The pitfalls of this "loving" ambiguity are not just related to language. The greater concern is that within the language of love there are any number of ways to enact hate, judgment, fear, and scarcity on the people around us, while still calling it a loving value. Telling Jewish people they are going to hell, for instance: but hey, it's just "speaking the truth in love." Or kicking a gay child out of the church or family while claiming to "love the sinner, but hate the sin."

That kind of love doesn't feel very loving. And yet, the word is the same.

It is one thing to verbally claim love as the root of a values system. It's another thing entirely to let compassion do the driving in everything, from our casual interactions to our most important relationships. But if we could learn to do just that, it would be a game changer—not just for our lives and families, but also for the world around us.

There's a word for love with skin on it: *compassion*.

Many communal values systems operate from that "love the sinner, hate the sin" perspective. Nuance that phrase any number of ways, but hate cannot abide that closely to love without fundamentally tarnishing love's good intentions. That is love that lives on the surface, but lacks arms and legs; love that is well-meaning, but still lets judgment do most of the talking.

On the surface, "family values" culture may look like warm, fuzzy stuff: Love, loyalty, and strong relationships. Start pulling on some of those threads, though, and we uncover the many ways in which love is limited, and relationships are rigidly defined—even confining. In any number of ways, love—in its vague abstractions—leaves a lot of room for hate to creep in around the edges. And not just hate—fear, rage, passive aggression, and any number of social ills that come from well-meaning sentimentality but ultimately become destructive forces in our lives and families.

Compassion, on the other hand, doesn't leave room for judgment or fear, or exclusion, or rigid parameters of belonging. Why? Because compassion is *work*. And those who are busy, every day, enacting compassion on the world have neither the time nor the brain space available for deciding who's in and who's out, for flinching at any sign of "otherness," or for the general shenanigans of moral posturing.

And this is where values have the power to reshape us and our world. When we can truly identify what our core values are—beyond abstraction, sound bites, and bumper stickers—they move to the center of our lives. When we nurture those values, they expand, leaving no space for that which tears down others, wastes our time, and distracts us from the holiness inherent in all things.

Our values system is naturally rooted in that which we love. Love is our primary human compass. But let love just sit there—a thing we feel, or a word we say—and so many other things can work their way into our lives and hearts. Compassion is the exercise by which that love takes on flesh in our own faith, our family, and the world.

My early morning rant in the car line might not be hurting anyone. It is not overtly hateful or harmful. But what I've come to realize—as I explore my values and the ways in which they can direct my life, home, and faith practice—is that the "harmless" anxiety and rage that crop up in these everyday moments are not entirely harmless after all.

For instance: I catch myself wanting to roll down the window and shout at one dad in a giant pickup truck, "You can't do that! You have to go to the back of the line like everyone else!" I want to lay on the horn (OK, sometimes I have laid on the horn) and wildly gesture that there is a *line* here, and you are straight-up breaking the first and primary rule of kindergarten: wait your eff'n turn, bro.

But, let's say that I allow myself to indulge that compulsion. I yell, I honk, I act like a deranged caricature of suburbia, but then, say, two weeks later, I realize that guy's kid is in my kid's class, and we are on the Halloween party planning committee together. Suddenly, I find that I don't want to be so involved in my kid's class this year after all. My momentary anger has damaged a longer term relationship—not just with this one family but with an entire network of families who will be in my kid's life this year.

What if this guy turns out to be my neighbor as well? Do I avoid his wife at the mailbox? Do I duck and not say hello at the grocery store? My entire communal environment has been disrupted by one unloving moment.

This is undesirable outcome number one, in a progressive family values system. The narrative that we want to build is not just a rejection of harmful, fundamentalist rhetoric—but a better, more life-giving story for our family and world. That work is primarily rooted in connectivity and the wholeness of humanity. Any fracture in that system, however small, contributes to the greater schisms that harm us all.

Add to that the missed opportunity to model grace and kindness for those little people in the backseat. What does this do to her playground behavior? His ability to play on a team? Their outlook on the world and its people as a whole?

A 10-second outburst can have a ripple effect—and not the good kind—on the way in which we engage the world. We all have these moments, and hopefully we can learn to extend some grace to even our worst selves on those days. But more importantly, we can use those darker moments to recognize that simple acts of compassion can also ripple, in a good way. In the best possible ways.

The truth is, anxiety or rage that crops up in an everyday kind of moment is really rushing in to fill a void. A void that I have enabled through my own lack of intention.

How can I fill that void with life-giving things instead?

What if we started taking the long view, every day? What if we cultivated the all-consuming mindfulness of knowing that each word or interaction affects our overall relationship potential? In a hundred small ways a day, we have the power to be intentional in the ways we engage our family, our neighbor, and the world around us. This is how we build a better narrative that is not just reactionary and prescriptive, but life-giving and transformative. And it starts here.

It starts, like God's mercies, new every morning. It starts with having a moment to breathe before I rush into the day, a moment to ground myself in the abiding love that I know lives within me, and can transform the world if I let it. It starts with being the kind of person each day that I want my kids to see me be. If I want them to know love that is more than words, I have to work on modeling that loving presence to our friends and neighbors. Even when it's not easy or obvious. Even when it may not make for a good bumper sticker.

PRACTICING COMPASSION AT HOME

Perhaps the best way to nurture the value of compassion is to encourage our children in that which they already love.

My daughter has been a vegetarian since she was four years old. The minute she found out where that pork chop came from, she started quietly saying "I don't eat meat" and pushing it away. We still included small portions on her plate for a while—until she started loudly declaring "*I DON'T EAT ANI-MALS!*" in restaurants.

This is a child who once obsessed for days about a lost cat poster she saw at the park. "Where will it sleep? How did it get lost? What if they don't find it? Can we please go look some more and take that cat home to its family?" This is the child who cried for hours when she saw a dog chained up in a yard, worried that it might be left outside overnight and get cold. This is the kid who is always first to run and take the leftover communion bread out to feed the birds.

She didn't get it from her parents. I mean, we like animals. Animals are great. We love our family dog, we want SeaWorld to be more humane, and we carefully read the animal-safety instructions at every national park we visit. But we love bacon. And cheeseburgers. There was nothing intentional on our part that would have caused our toddler to develop the heart of Saint Francis. But it is the heart she has, and so we do our best to care for it.

When we encourage her in that which she already loves, it becomes a compassionate way of life that will shape how she interacts with the world. I try to involve her in SAGE, our church's environmental ministry. I introduce her to people who are connected with animal advocacy and preservation efforts. They send her reading material about a wolf rescue place in New Mexico. We go to the library for animal books. And yes, we let her be a vegetarian. Even at age four, five, now eight and someday eighteen. Even if it means making something extra for dinner so she has enough protein; even if it means the rest of us make an effort to eat less meat.

In this way, she is beginning to shape the world around her—even within her own household, where we now try to eat meat only twice a week. In addition to just supporting her, there are also significant environmental and economic reasons to eat less meat. And a child shall lead them.

Speaking of food—my boy child loves food. *Loves* it. Ever since he was a baby. In fact, from the time he could eat solid food until the time he could effectively feed himself, we could not eat in a restaurant because he would sit in his high chair and scream bloody murder in between bites. We literally could not shovel it in fast enough for him, and if somebody else was chewing and there was not food in, or on the way to, his mouth, there was hell to pay. So for nearly a year, there was only home cooking on the menu.

Once he got to be about 18 months old and he could feed himself a slice of pizza (or rather, a whole pizza), then all was right in the world. He is the most well-behaved kid in the restaurant now, because if there's food, he is happy.

He doesn't just love to eat. He loves to go grocery shopping. He loves to look at recipes on the computer with me, and he loves to cook. When he was about 3, I realized that he could put all the groceries away *by himself*, and he loved to do it. He was so happy going through the bags to see what I got. "Cinnamon rolls!" he would call to his sister. "Mommy got cinnamon rolls! And apples! And yogurt!" The kid loves food (and speaking in exclamation marks).

Perhaps he did come by this foodie spirit by way of his parents. In any case, it is an easy love to nurture, in many ways. Yes, he helps with the groceries and he will hopefully be cooking us dinner in the foreseeable future. But we try to harness his love of food in ways that can be turned outward as well.

Our neighborhood food bank is one of the few places in our area that allows young children to volunteer. So on many a Friday morning we spend a couple hours sorting and packaging food for other people at "the food helping place." He may or may not understand the premise—that some people don't have enough to eat, and we want to help them—but he definitely understands food. Sorting frozen french fries into plastic baggies, tossing the broken eggs and salvaging the keepers, organizing boxes of cereal and pasta—this kid is in his element.

Meanwhile, my husband is teaching him the joys of gardening—a new endeavor at our house. As they both learn the art of bringing edibles up from the ground, my son is connecting two of his great loves—food and Dad—with ways of caring for the earth. He is also getting to do fun things like composting. We call him the sheriff, because he does not mess around. "Don't throw that away!" he shouts, as he polices the trash bins.

Whether or not he understands the significance of what he is doing at this young age, he is learning compassionate ways of living, as it applies to his favorite thing in life: food. Just as my daughter is learning that her love for animals can have outward, global expressions. I trust that encouraging them in what already sits close to their hearts will ultimately shape their character, their connective abilities, and the hopeful ways in which they approach the world.

Maybe someday, I will find that I'm the mother of an environmentalist and a humanitarian aid worker. Maybe between the two of them they will save the planet and end world hunger.

Or maybe they will be a vet and a chef who are kind to their neighbors. I'll call it a win, either way.

We may not always know how to "teach" compassion to a child. But we do know how to stoke the fires of what they already love. We know how to model compassion in ordinary, everyday ways. And every now and then, we catch a glimpse of what it looks like when that value has effectively taken root in a child's being.

Teaching compassion is not a list of behaviors. It is a way of moving through the world. And moving through the world as compassionate people is not just the work of raising children. It is the work of our faith. It is the work that transforms, and puts flesh on the gospel.

My friend Annie writes beautifully about life with her son Collin. Collin has a genetic disease, one that is rare and mostly a mystery. She recently shared this story, about an ordinary day:

> I have to admit, when the older lady signaled that she wanted to ask me a question, I sighed inside. It felt like we had been riding a wave of Collin interactions ranging

from uncomfortable to hurtful. Lots of "What's wrong with him?" and "Please list everything he will and won't be able to do for the rest of his life."

But when I kneeled down so I could hear her over the splashing and yelling, she said, "Can I ask you: how would you prefer me to talk to my grandkids about your son?"

I looked over at Collin. His hair stood up in a dripping fin and his face shone with the joy of being weightless in the water. The woman's red-haired grandchildren crowded close around him and the aquatherapist, glued to his every move as they tried to figure out what exactly they were seeing.

"Would you use the word 'special'?" she went on. "Would you say he has special needs? Is that a term you're comfortable with?"

I may have visibly expanded with gratitude. This woman knew that words were important. She could have said anything she wanted without me ever knowing, but she knew it mattered how she talked about Collin. It mattered for her grandkids, for Collin, and for me.

I told her to tell them that his name is Collin. That he has disabilities which, for him, means that a lot of the things other kids his age can easily do, he can't do yet.

Her grandson had sidled up quietly. "Like swimming?" he asked.

I smiled. "No, actually he's really good at swimming. It's other things like talking and walking he has trouble with."

He nodded and returned to Collin. I introduced them. They were both six years old. And, like some kind of soaking wet miracle, the little boy reached out and they shook hands.[1]

We may not be able to put an easy list of bullet points around the work of compassion, but we know the fruits of that labor when we see it. In this story, we see what it looks like when children have taken note of the daily practice of active compassion, and mirror that behavior back to us. That's how the values we model at home in small, daily ways take shape in the world around us.

PRACTICING COMPASSION IN COMMUNITY

My neighbors, Courtney and Stephanie, wanted to find intentional ways for their families to serve the community. The challenge is that most nonprofits don't allow volunteers under a certain age. Feeling strongly that the roots of compassion need to be planted in early childhood, these two moms took another approach. They started planning age-appropriate ways for young school age children to help others, and to learn more about the needs present in their community.

For their first few activities—like making blankets for patients at a children's hospital—they involved a few other families. But they realized that many other families shared their desire to do something active, but didn't always know where to start. So they planned a toiletry drive for a local mission, and invited all the families in our school to participate. In order to create a more hands-on experience, they planned an evening gathering for the kids to organize the donations and assemble toiletry kits.

The response was overwhelming. Over 200 people showed up for that first event. Before all was said and done, it was not just a neighborhood thing. Thanks to the wonders of social media, friends—and friends of friends—got involved.

In just a few months, that first big event evolved into a nonprofit, aptly named KindCraft[2] (think "Minecraft," with a clever pixilated logo). The name, like the group itself, evolved out of a desire to build a compassionate lifestyle in families and in neighborhood communities. This movement grew quickly from two families to many, drawing in people from different churches, neighborhoods, and scout troops.

The rapid growth of this new organization shows a real hunger present in most of our communities. People genuinely want to serve, to model compassionate living for their children, and to give life to their corner of the world. People also want to know their neighbors better, even if much of our culture speaks to growing isolation and the worship of autonomy.

When we answer the desire to serve others and the need to feel rooted in our place, then we are acknowledging an important truth of human experience, and a central philosophy of progressive values—*it's not just about us.* We are only as strong as the community in which we live, and we, ourselves, are strengthened in community.

This is where vital communities of faith, and even neighborhood groups can truly find their power and relevance in our current context. When we can connect (1) the fundamental need for community and (2) the deep desire for meaning and purpose, we have unlocked the heart of the gospel. Individuals grow in faith, families are strengthened, and the local community becomes an extension of that compassionate spirit.

As in other forms of learning, tactile, hands-on experience is the best teacher. We want people of all ages in our families and churches to grow in a spirit of love, service, and outward thinking; and that spirit is most firmly rooted in practice.

Even in the car line.

COMPASSION IN SCRIPTURE

Surprisingly, the word "compassion" doesn't appear much in English translations of Scripture. One of the few places it does occur is in the story of the Prodigal Son.

In Luke 15:11–32, a son has abandoned his family's values and cashed in his inheritance early in order to go on a journey of what can only be called youthful hedonism. Predictably, he blows it all in Vegas (or the biblical equivalent thereof): wine, women, gambling, fast cars, the works. Finding himself cold, hungry, and sleeping among the pigs, he does what errant kids have done since the beginning of time: he wonders if he can go home again. Will he be accepted in this shameful state? Or has too much been lost? Perhaps they will just send him off to sleep in his filth. It's what he would deserve, after all.

The good news—for him, and for wandering youth every-where—is that real love is not about deserving. As he winds his way up that driveway, head hung in shame and stomach aching with hunger, his father greets him "with compassion," the Scripture tells us; with joyful abandon.

This is not just passive acceptance: *Okay, I guess you can sleep in the barn and earn your keep.* This is not a passive-aggressive exercise in "Loving the sinner, hating the sin," by which the father takes the son back but constantly reminds him of his wrongdoing. This father pursues active compassion. This is love, embodied and mobile.

How can this father be so "filled with compassion" when, clearly, what that boy needs is a good head-thumping? Or at the very least, to have his iPhone taken away for eternity. That's certainly what his brother would like to see happen. (Then again, how many of us would even be here right now, if our siblings had been allowed to decide our fate in matters of justice and discipline?)

But the satisfying, well-deserved ass-kicking is not what we witness. Instead, we hear a story of transformative love. Mercy, forgiveness, and radical acceptance change the boy's life direction more than any act of discipline ever could. The boy who broke his heart; the boy who took what he wanted and left, thinking of none but himself; and yet, here we witness the pure joy of a parent whose child has come home.

The father and the brother in this story represent two different ways of being family. There is the brother's way—the way of responding to baser impulses and holding onto grudges; the way of indignant outrage and "it's my turn," and "that's not fair." It is, ultimately, the way of dwelling in what's been lost.

Or, there is the father's way: the way of loving with abandon, extending undeserved mercy; it is the way of running down the driveway, the way of "bring up the fatted calf" and "put the best sheets on his old bed" and "wherever you've been, whatever you've done, we only care that you are here now."

That is the way of compassion. And it is a core value of the faith that we share, and the strong, loving families that we hope to raise.

Scripture is full of dysfunctional families—abuse and rejection, lies and betrayal, neglect and violence and retribution—but we also find instances of love embodied; the radical roots of belonging that overcome any wrongdoing or wayward wandering. Our call is to model this *radical rooting* in our families and faith communities. Exhibiting compassion, not just in an everyday kind of way, but at the moment when it feels the most counterintuitive. Of course, there are moments for discipline, and there are times when natural consequences can be the greatest teacher. But there are also days—most of the days, when we think about it—when the work of compassion holds the greater powers of transformation.

Perhaps the best, most important ministry we can do—as parents, and as the Church—is to raise compassionate children. In daily, intentional ways, we impart this value to the kids in our circles: not just as a spark of verbal wisdom, but as a truth that they know in the core of their being. Rooted in radical, embodied love, they will know beyond doubt that they can always come home, and will always be loved and accepted. If we watch closely, we'll see that they approach their world in this same compassionate way.

AROUND THE TABLE: QUESTIONS FOR DISCUSSION

1. What passion does your child possess that could be nurtured into an active compassion? What passions of your own could be focused outward?
2. When have you heard "love" expressed in a way that might not be very loving in spirit? How might you reframe that perspective and shape it into something more life-giving?

3. Where do you meet your greatest challenge to compassionate living?
4. How does your church, family, or local community engage in acts of compassion? Do you see evidence of this practice or activity in the world around you?

2
Abundance: The Root of Gratitude and Generosity

I followed a sparkly red ladybug and a plush green dragon down the street.

Never mind that it was October 31. It was about 100 degrees outside and the plush, fuzzy, cozy costume—which would have been just swell in some chilly autumn Midwestern borough—was utterly ridiculous in the desert. But he sure was adorable.

We'd just moved from one desert suburb to another—just a few miles apart, but worlds away. The place we'd been the previous year—with a two-year-old witch and a newborn—had proved a little disappointing on Halloween. We only knocked on about eight doors, and of those, only two actually opened and produced candy.

There was a reason that neighborhood was a ghost town, and it had nothing to do with Halloween. In 2008, the bottom dropped out of the Phoenix housing market. It was one of the hardest-hit areas in the country, and it led to a mass exodus from the valley. I don't know if our neighborhood was a direct reflection of the metro-wide trend, but about one in three houses on our block was in short sale or foreclosure by 2010;

ours included. There was no one handing out candy that year because those houses were abandoned. It was a little spooky but not in a festive way.

A year later, the economy had begun the slow crawl of recovery. And trick-or-treat, in our new neighborhood, was an *event*. We had a potluck on the cul-de-sac, took group pics of the kids, and then went trick-or-treating en masse. Our group had about eight kids and twice as many parents. And every street we went down, we encountered another mob of kids and their chaperones. Nearly every house was decorated, every porch light on, every resident proffering a giant bowl of tiny treats.

Thirty minutes later, my furry monster was burning up, and both of their buckets were full. The little ladybug could no longer carry her load, and I was picking up the trail of M&M'S packets accumulating behind her. I announced that, since the buckets were full, we were calling it a night.

But one of the other moms said, "Oh, this always happens, so we come prepared." And she pulled out a handful of empty plastic grocery bags and started handing them around.

So . . . we did another block of houses. Then another.

Don't get me wrong. It was great fun. And I like digging through the buckets, post-bedtime, and hijacking all the Snickers as much as the next mom. But at some point, we've got to acknowledge that the bucket is *full*, and go home already.

But sometimes we lose that inner voice. The one that tells us, "This is all you need, you can stop now." It's still in there, somewhere, but we have a hard time hearing it.

The much louder fear of "not enough" whispers anxiety in our ear at every turn. It is the real goblin that haunts us all the year around; maybe, even especially, in the holiday season. It snatches our happiest moments sometimes and fills us with dread. Sometimes, it even tries to take hold of our children.

That voice of scarcity had a lot to do with what happened to the Phoenix housing market, in general, and to our house, specifically.

Not to overwork the metaphor, but had the big banks just gone home when their bucket was full, there would not have been such an economic crisis to begin with. Corporate greed rendered our home—and that of so many others—worthless, overnight.

This is an apt illustration, but corporations are certainly not the only ones vulnerable to that myth of scarcity, in some broad cultural abstraction. At some point I had to acknowledge that same voice had shaped our own family decisions. Did I buy a "solid investment" narrative so thoroughly that I didn't mind paying an inflated price for that vague future stability? Was I in such a hurry to feel settled and secure that I didn't ask enough questions about what could go wrong in a market so saturated with new construction and unchecked expansion?

I knew, deep down, that the answer to both of these questions was "yes."

There was a lot of judgment and shame coming from the public at large during that time—directed not at banks but at homeowners. Most people assumed that the "victims" of the housing crisis were irresponsible young people (or self-indulgent older ones) who bought houses they couldn't afford, took on too much debt, and ultimately bailed on the payments when it got to be too much.

That's not how it was.

How it was—at least in Phoenix—was that we (and lots of our neighbors) bought a modest house at an inflated, but good-for-the-market-at-the-time price. A starter home or investment property, most would have called it. Small (not much bigger than an apartment) but in a good area. For us, the payments were totally doable. But then the bottom dropped out. And many of us who had paid what was "fair market price" for our modest homes woke up one morning to find that our homes were worth nothing.

That's what is called a bad debt. We stayed for nearly four more years without missing a payment—until we finally acknowledged that every payment on this loan was throwing good money after bad. We finally qualified for a short sale, which was a fairly new, evolving option at that time, and no one seemed able to tell us what the long-term effects would be. But at least we had people who could help us navigate the system in a new landscape. In many ways, we just exchanged one uncertain future for another.

We moved into a nice rental home where the rent cost a fraction of what it would have cost us a few years before. (In fact, rental property was scarce when we moved to town— which is mostly why we bought a home in the first place.) But we still felt displaced. And the truly heartbreaking thing was that the bank sold our house for a fraction—less than half—of what we had paid just a few years before.

Of course, *we* could have kept the house at that price. But it doesn't work that way.

In the end, we were grateful to get out of there with our shirts (and our credit) mostly intact. But it truly felt like being robbed.

And yet, somehow, those desert years were a lesson in abundance. When I remember the ghost town feel of the suburban neighborhoods at that time, I think not of what I lost but how I learned to find connectedness, roots, and belonging in other ways.

The art of finding abundance—even in the midst of seeming scarcity—is the foundation of cultivating generosity.

Global activist and fundraising guru Lynn Twist writes about shifting perspective in *The Soul of Money.* She says:

> For me, and for many of us, my first waking thought of the day is "I didn't get enough sleep." The next one is "I don't have enough time." Whether true or not, that thought of "not enough" occurs to us automatically before we even think to question or examine it. We spend most of the hours and the days of our lives hearing, explaining, complaining, or worrying about what we don't have enough of. We don't have enough time. We don't have enough rest. We don't have enough exercise. We don't have enough work. We don't have enough profits. We don't have enough power. We don't have enough wilderness. We don't have enough weekends. Of course, we don't have enough money—ever. Before we even sit up in bed, before our feet touch the floor, we're already inadequate, already

behind, already losing, already lacking something. And by
the time we go to bed at night, our minds race with a litany
of what we didn't get, or didn't get done, that day. We go
to sleep burdened by those thoughts and wake up to the
reverie of lack. This mantra of "not enough" carries the
day and becomes a kind of default setting for our thinking
about everything.[1]

I re-read parts of this book every year as my congregation
begins the annual process of budgeting, and raising funds to
support the budget. I find it both convicting and refreshing,
every single time. Like a light shined on a particular darkness.
The darkness is unsettling, but the light also offers an invitation to a better way.

As a parent, I find that practicing abundance is not as simple as teaching kids the value of money, or teaching them that
"we tithe because the Bible says we should." When our lives
are so full of stuff, and so full of mixed messages about human
worth, then navigating the cultural landmines of materialism
takes a bit more finesse than just whipping out the Bible and
the checkbook.

It is certainly important to teach kids the value of money,
and the responsibility to share out of our abundance to serve
others. Teaching them what things cost, how to be responsible
and save, how to postpone gratification and plan ahead—all
that is central to fiscal upbringing.

But there's a fine line sometimes between teaching the value
of money and unintentionally transferring a sense of scarcity.
If we aren't intentional about placing abundance at the heart
of that conversation, a looming sense of scarcity can move in
to fill the void. We can be good savers and still be misers—as
Ebenezer Scrooge and all his real-life, modern-day expressions
remind us. How do we build a family system that is rooted not
just in "responsibility," but in an abiding trust in God's provision and care? How do we build a deep sense of belonging and
connectedness that will transcend any circumstance of housing, employment, or transition?

It begins with teaching them to say "enough," even as the world says, "here's an extra bag so you can carry more stuff." That Halloween season several years ago was an important transitional time in our lives, and I learned a lot about simply breathing it all in, and being grateful for what is. In other seasons of transition—from one church call to another, from the desert to the prairie, from caring for babies to parenting big(ish) kids—that breath of gratitude is a liturgy of rest and belonging.

After trick-or-treating on block after block that night, I hauled a loaded bucket, a full-to-breaking plastic bag, and some exhausted kids home. I was grateful for my new neighborhood; for doors that actually opened in welcome, for a roof over my family's head, for healthy kids who could eat candy . . . and for those fleeting years of glitter and wings and magic.

Out of the overflow, I handed my ladybug two pieces of candy and I said, *"Repeat after me: this is enough. This is all we need."*

PRACTICING ABUNDANCE AT HOME

You know what was great about living in the desert all those years? Among other things—not having to wear socks. Maybe occasionally we would don socks with running shoes or hiking boots if we were going out on a trail, because of the rattlesnakes. But otherwise, it was ten months a year of sandals. Glorious, breezy, open-toed, sockless *freedom.*

This was heaven, because the only thing worse than wearing socks is *finding socks.* I mean, what happens to them? Where do they possibly go? They go *on* feet, they don't *have* feet! Why do I spend so many winter (and fall, and spring, now that we live in a more temperate clime) mornings digging through drawers, only to come up with sad, single socklings? I have trouble enough keeping my own feet clothed. Coming up with socks for two children? *Every day?* Forget about matching; I will settle for clean(ish). But combine the mysterious disappearing properties of socks with the hoarding tendencies of my kids and, have mercy, I am only one person. A person who hates socks.

After yet another morning of the sock-hunt dance, as I was about to pick up yet another pack of the dreaded articles for each kid at Costco, I stopped myself. *This is crazy. I just bought socks. And they did not leave my house of their own accord.* We might joke about people who buy new underwear rather than doing laundry, but I often buy new socks rather than hunt down the ones I know we already own. This is wasteful. Not just wasteful of our family's money, but wasteful in a more global, environmentally ominous kind of way. Americans generate more than 10 million tons of textile waste each year.[2]

So on that day, I made a conscious decision not to throw another dozen pair of socks on the pile. Instead, I went home and staged a scavenger hunt. I told the kids I'd give them 10 cents for every sock they could find. I sent them to look under beds and dressers; to dig in the couch cushions; to mine the bottom of the toy box. I sent them to the basement, the garage, the backseats of our cars. They combed the backyard and the back of the closet.

Two competing piles formed in the hallway. The race was on. At one point, I was shouting to my son, "Your sister's got more than you! Find one more sock and you get a whole dollar!"

Fifteen minutes later, we had twelve pairs of socks. Matching, even. They earned a dollar a piece, and I didn't have to buy more stuff.

There's a parable in there, somewhere . . . some profound spiritual truth about how much of what we need is already ours, and we just have to dig through the junk to find it. But more practically speaking, it's a literal lesson in keeping up with the damn stuff we've already got, before we go buy more damn stuff.

This exercise opened my eyes (and hopefully my kids' eyes) to how often we really do go buy stuff that we already have. I take this scavenger hunt approach to all sorts of things now before I buy more: cold medicine, crayons and markers, hair ties, hats and gloves—truly, how many gloves can we possibly lose in a season? What about food? How many cans of beans, Spaghettios, and/or cream of mushroom soup can one pantry hide in its darkest corners? How many notebooks have I started but not finished? *How many phone chargers can one household hold?* It's a whole new world. Scavenger Hunt Mondays are the new Taco Tuesday. Before making a grocery list, we shop the pantry. Before every trip to Target or the neighborhood yard sale, we sift through our junk and acknowledge how much we already have.

Another good practice for teaching kids the art of abundance: don't let them hear us worry about money. Don't let them hear arguments over money. Don't let them hear anxiety about how parents are going to pay for camp, college, the medical bills. There will be time enough to teach them about budgeting and fiscal responsibility. For now, for this blessed season of childhood—teach them abundance. Teach "enough."

Language matters. If they ask for something at the store, my first impulse is often, "We can't afford that," or "That costs too much money." But what does that really teach them? It is one more subtle message that *we don't have enough.* Isn't the better lesson, "We don't need that"? Or more specifically, *"We already have everything that we need"?*

That simple liturgy—on repeat in our households—might be the most countercultural message we can instill in our children. *We have everything that we need.*

My kids don't often ask for "stuff," because they know that unless it is Christmas, birthday, or vacation (for which they save and spend their own money on stuff) they are probably not going to get it. But when they do ask, I've tried to reframe my default response. Instead of "Do you know how much that costs?" or "Do you think money grows on trees?" I try to dial down the scarcity speak, and say instead, "We don't really need that." Or, "We have something a lot like that already." (Or,

"If you really want that, let's talk about some extra chores or spending your birthday money.")

I don't know that it makes a big difference, in the grand scheme of things. But I can't help but think, in a world that surrounds them with "you need more" and "you are never enough," these subtle reminders will, ultimately, sink in and create a resistance. A powerful, alternative response to the world's epidemic of scarcity.

And of course, people who *believe* that they have enough actually do have more. It is not just self-fulfilling prophecy; it is a practical reality. People who always note abundance spend less of their money, time, and energy running around trying to fill the void with new and different things. Resources are freed up for experiences—traveling to new places, trying new things, spending time together as a family, going to visit people we love.

The liturgy of "enough" needs to be more than just spoken. Beyond just articulating this value, we model the truth of abundance in the ways we consume—and choose not to consume—every day. We can refrain from exhibiting anxiety about the thing that we want but can't afford. And we can celebrate the many ways that we have more than enough by sharing that abundance with others.

Shaping life around the value of abundance leaves more room for giving to others; more gifts to share with the church, more to help the poor, more to contribute to causes that a family can gather around and feel good about supporting together. In fact, this whole conversation about values-based living can help your family decide what services and organizations best reflect your shared priorities. Identifying those efforts and groups you want to support can provide a shared sense of purpose.

Noting abundance and practicing generosity together as a family will yield multiple benefits. Not only will your family feel more connected, you will notice lots of everyday anxieties diminish with your growing outward focus. The mantras of "we have enough," "we have everything that we need," and "what do I already have to be grateful for?" put so many things in perspective. You might even find that it changes your pace; maybe there are fewer errands to run, fewer bills to pay, less "stuff" to manage in general.

Between the circumstances of our Phoenix housing situation and ministry life in general—plus the fact that we're just kind of nomads at heart—my family has moved a lot. My husband and I have lived in eight different places in thirteen years of marriage and our kids have lived in five of those. Granted, some of those places were short-term, transitional things while we found something more permanent. But it all adds up to shifting lots of stuff. Each time we move, we do a major—and I mean *major*—purge. We cast off anything that we can live without, anything that might not work in our new space, and really, anything that we haven't used in the past year.

As a result, we have way less stuff than the average suburban family of four. But it's also been an extremely tedious task, every single time, to sift through all those layers of civilization and rapid childhood growth; tedious and emotionally exhausting. Even being intentional about how much (or little) comes through our doors, life happens. And the next time we move, I'm sure life will have "happened" again, and we'll be back in the same boat.

What I do know is that, each time we start fresh in a new place, having filtered much of the chaos out of our personal space, we feel a kind of lightness. Once we've unpacked, there is a kind of order to everything that feels simple and good and freeing. We try, as much as possible, to hang onto that renewed sense of simplicity, and in as many ways as we can. Until, of course, school starts and paper starts piling up on the counters. Again.

The point, though, is not just to free up physical space—although disciples of the popular book *The Life-Changing Magic of Tidying Up* will say that is the key to the universe. It's more about cultivating the life-altering art of "enough." When we know, in the core of our being, that we have enough, we can maybe start to believe that we *are* enough. Just as we are. And that changes everything.

PRACTICING ABUNDANCE IN COMMUNITY

What kind of story do we want our lives to tell?

I think of the beautiful Christmas letters that some people compose and send out to friends and family. Or the creative, thoughtfully organized scrapbooks, filled with meaningful photos, funny stories, and wonderful memories shared in the year before.

Notice I wrote "some people." Such organized archiving has never been, shall we say, my spiritual gift. I occasionally sift through my photos online in case we want to print them. Someday. Maybe. But I so appreciate the time and energy that others are able to put into crafting the family narrative. I wonder if the rest of us mortals can find other ways to craft that family narrative—not in literal letter or scrapbook form, but rather in living the story we would want such an archive to tell. Might that story be reflected in the things that fill our homes? Or maybe the things that don't? Could our story be witnessed by way of the bank statement, the charitable giving on our tax returns, or maybe even the kinds of experiences that we deem worth our investment of time and money?

Now take that lived story, and extend it out into the wider community. No matter how many times we repeat the mantra at home—*we have enough*—it will not truly sink in unless it is reinforced by the village. How can the communities of which we are a part tell stories of abundance, rather than stories of scarcity?

Many faith-based organizations are adopting the narrative budget approach that other nonprofits have employed for years in their fundraising practices.[3] The narrative budget is like the family Christmas letter. Traditionally, churches have passed around the pledge cards and said, "Here's how much we need to pay the bills—and we need your help!" That works, to a point. But what other organizations—from higher education to the local food bank—have known for a long time is that people are far more likely to support a story of abundance than one of scarcity. Rather than just going over the line-item budget and hoping that people will give out of a sense of duty, the narrative approach is to tell the story first. The community, with a shared sense of ownership in the mission, can then work to faithfully live into it, together.

Think of it this way. Let's say there are two similar organizations in a community that work to support homeless families. They each send out an "ask" letter in the fall, along with a pledge card. One letter includes the organization's mission statement, along with a line-item budget and a few paragraphs about how hard it is to operate with limited resources. There is a run-down of utility costs, building overhead, staff salaries, and maybe a little anecdote about how many families have received services from the organization in the last year.

But the other program's letter begins with the anecdote. And it's not statistical, it is narrative. It's the story of one family, and how a series of circumstances led them into poverty. How they found this agency at exactly the right moment, when they were all out of options. How, with the support of the local community, this family was able to stay together, find secure, sustainable housing, and develop a plan to move forward. This family is now volunteering with said local agency, and working to help other families in need, just like they once were.

We have helped <u>62</u> other families, just like this one, in the past year. With your continued support, we hope to reach <u>85</u> families in the year ahead. This is the ending of the second letter, and recipients are already reaching for their checkbooks without even flipping to the next page to scan the line-item budget and the breakdown of operating costs.

The first letter has already made its way to the recycling bin, the organization's name already forgotten.

I probably don't need to point out which letter a church is more likely to send out.

Approaching the budget as a story of shared mission and future hope is an exercise in abundance; one that enables leaders to *begin with the story they want to be living,* rather than beginning each year, each quarter, each meeting with a report on what's in the bank (or, more often, what's not in the bank). Financial reports are still important for transparency and actual operations—but beginning with the story of who we want to be is a way of moving past the world's scale of worth and success, practicing gratitude, and choosing God's path of wholeness and plenty.

It's profoundly ironic, then, that churches often suffer from "scarcity speak" more than any other organization in the history of the world. Go to any church finance meeting, sit through an annual stewardship campaign, or sift through years' worth of board meeting minutes—and it will be apparent that "*we don't have enough*" is the unofficial mission statement for many a congregation.

That constant angst seeps into the church from the culture at large, but is also upheld by bad religion. The idea that there is *not enough* grace for everyone lies at the heart of a traditional values narrative, and roots the entire system in that spirit. That God's mercy is somehow not big enough to include our Muslim or LGBT neighbors; that salvation can only be found through a narrowly prescribed path of prescribed language and activity; that family only functions within rigid parameters and gender roles. These are all riffs on the same story of scarcity, and can be deeply harmful to family connections, as well as the individual spirit.

So it's no surprise when declining numbers in worship attendance (and dollars in the offering plate, accordingly) lead to more "not enoughs." Not enough money, not enough people, not enough volunteers. Or it can go quite the other way too. The minute a church begins to experience growth, there is not enough staff, not enough classrooms, not enough chairs in the fellowship hall, and so on. And we're back on this endless treadmill, dwelling on what we lack instead of on all that God has provided.

The only way for a faith community to overcome that narrative is to cultivate an alternate story. An intentional identity rooted in the mantra that "we have everything we need." And, thankfully, many churches in our contemporary context are learning how to do just that. For some churches, it means selling the building—letting go of the property that is too big for a shrinking membership, or in need of expensive repairs, or no longer meeting the needs of a growing organization. Some churches—whether starting over or just starting out—are realizing how much more mission and community building can be done when resources (and collective energy) are not being poured into facilities management.

There is no one way to cultivate a healthy sense of abundance in a community. Much like adopting an abundance mindset as a family, a church that begins its own story in the provision of God and the many gifts of community will find that it does, in fact, have enough. That shared story comes to serve as both a mission focus tool and a valuable messaging snapshot for new members. A community with a shared purpose and vision—much like a family that is unified around its values—will be more connected, more functional, and always more ready to share its gifts with others.

Once a community has begun to root itself in the art of abundant living, it can be more intentional about reinforcing "enough" with its children. The church that I serve has always included children and youth in the annual giving campaign. I take no credit for this practice, as it predates my tenure—but I have been impressed by the kind of dialogue it creates within the congregation, as well as the teaching moment it provides for families.

When the "ask" letters go out to our adult members, children receive a letter and a pledge card of their own. Their letters, like the grown-up versions, contain some theological teaching about *why* we give—not because we have to, but because we are grateful for all that God has given us. The letter also shares *what* we do with the money—to promote understanding of how a church works, and why our support matters. And, most importantly, the letters talk about *more ways of giving than just money.* We talk with our children about the gifts of prayer, caring for others, leading in worship, singing, creating artwork and sending cards, and even just showing up for church. The pledge cards that we collect each year ask our members, of all ages, what gifts they will share in the coming year. The blank space to write in a dollar amount is one of many spaces on the card. The goal is to reinforce that message that *our money is not who we are; and who we are is exactly what the church needs.* We have enough; we are enough. This cannot be overstated.

ABUNDANCE IN SCRIPTURE

It's all right there in Genesis. At the first breath of creation, God filled the world with good things. Living, moving, breathing, colorful, joyful, abundant life. The garden, the skies, and the seas were all filled with the goodness of God. And people were created with no other purpose but to enjoy it, and to honor God by caring for it.

It's pretty much all downhill from there.

That story of abundance is the first, what, two chapters? Then the rest of Genesis—and really, the rest of the Bible—is the story of human resistance to God's definition of plenty.

Walter Brueggemann's timeless essay on "The Liturgy of Abundance, the Myth of Scarcity" points out that initial fullness and wholeness of all that God created.

The Bible starts out with a liturgy of abundance. Genesis 1 is a song of praise for God's generosity. It tells how well the world is ordered. It keeps saying, "It is good, it is good, it is good, it is very good." It declares that God blesses—that is, endows with vitality—the plants and the animals and the fish and the birds and humankind. And it pictures the creator as saying, "Be fruitful and multiply." In an orgy of fruitfulness, everything in its kind is to multiply the overflowing goodness that pours from God's creator spirit. And as you know, the creation ends in Sabbath. God is so overrun with fruitfulness that God says, "I've got to take a break from all this. I've got to get out of the office. . . ."

Later in Genesis God blesses Abraham, Sarah and their family. God tells them to be a blessing, to bless the people of all nations. Blessing is the force of well-being active in the world, and faith is the awareness that creation is the gift that keeps on giving. That awareness dominates Genesis until its 47th chapter. In that chapter Pharaoh dreams that there will be a famine in the land. So Pharaoh gets organized to administer, control and monopolize the food supply. Pharaoh introduces the principle of scarcity into the world economy. For the first time in the Bible, someone says, "There's not enough. Let's get everything."[4]

I re-read this piece every fall as well, as I prepare to lead a church through another cycle of budgeting, fundraising, and giving thanks. It is a blessed cycle, but one so often fraught with anxiety, tension, and loaded history. I find that immersing myself in that "liturgy" puts me in a better place to lead through those landmines of "not enough," and engage in the spiritual exercise of pointing out abundance.

Brueggemann says that Pharaoh is the first to introduce scarcity to the world economy. But really—don't we witness it sooner than that? For example:

— Adam and Eve take that first bite of the apple because everything else in the garden suddenly seems like "not enough."
— Cain murders his brother because half of his parents' love and land and stuff is not enough for him.
— Abraham impregnates the slave Hagar—with the blessing of his wife Sarah—because God's promise that they will have a son is not enough for them.
— Jacob usurps his brother's blessing, because his share of the inheritance was not going to be enough.

All Scripture moves in this call-and-response kind of pattern: God provides; people doubt the sufficiency of that provision; people rely, instead, on their own cunning/brute strength/general awesomeness. Chaos ensues. Repeat.

Sometimes God gets royally pissed, in very Old Testament kinds of ways, but more often than not, God's response to human faithlessness is *more faithfulness.* More abundance. Blessing upon blessing. Manna-from-the-sky, twelve-tribes-of-sons, loaves-and-fishes kinds of blessing. Ridiculously lavish kinds of blessing.

You'd think we would know this story by now.

Imagine how different the world would be if all of God's people knew about the "enoughness" of creation. It would be back to the garden again. No poverty, no war, no destruction of the environment . . . and no casting out of the other.

It's worth noting that the Bible references homosexuality a grand total of six times (or twenty-something, if you include references to "man and wife" as proof texts to establish a heteronormative world order). But whether it's six or twenty, those references pale in comparison to how often the Bible references money. More than 2,000 times. That's how much more God cares about our sense of well-being and our spirit of generosity than about who "shall lie with" who.

That said, money is just one expression of our whole approach to abundance. Or rather, it is just one way of expressing our understanding of God's kind of abundance. When I think about Scriptures for teaching kids about generosity, giving thanks, and understanding God's provision, I don't go first to the money texts. The widow's mite is great and all, but there is much deeper narrative potential in the miracle stories. Jesus turning water to wine, or feeding the multitudes; Jesus telling the disciples to fish out of the other side of the dang boat, and the disciples finding that trust in him yields a miraculous catch; Israelites being fed in the wilderness; banquet parables; stories of life and health restored; or an outcast being drawn back into community—this is what happens in miracle stories. With Jesus, it's never just about the physical healing.

The story of God's abundant generosity to us—and our subsequent call to live graciously and generously—is woven through all of Scripture. But it is not limited to Scripture. Beyond words on the page, that narrative of God's radical provision continues to play out in our lives every day, when we are ready to notice it.

While it's important to teach children about money—for practical reasons as well as theological ones—cultivating an awareness of abundance is ground zero for any healthy relationship with our stuff and the people around us.

We can teach kids about filling out a pledge card, putting a coin in the basket, and helping with the food drive. All that is important. But building communities and families around the *liturgy of abundance* touches everything—from the health of our own savings accounts, to the contentment we find at home and in community; from the vitality of congregations to the well-being of our environment. If we start there, we can trust that the rest will follow. Grateful kids, connected families, and generous communities of faith.

It's all right there, in God's first creative word.

AROUND THE TABLE:
QUESTIONS FOR DISCUSSION

1. What are some of the messages of scarcity that you receive on a daily basis?
2. How does your family practice gratitude and generosity?
3. How does your faith community embody the "liturgy of abundance"? Or if your church lives in a pattern of scarcity, what language or practices might begin to change that pattern?
4. What is your favorite biblical story of abundance? What does it teach you about living generously?

3

Sabbath: Reclaiming Time to Be, and Be Together

We are dressed. We are sunscreened. We have the bags packed with all the snacks, all the sand toys, all the towels and water bottles and every imaginable accessory needed for a day at the beach.

"Do you have to pee?" I ask for the eighth time.

"*No*," he swears for the tenth.

You can see where this is going, right?

Two blocks later—halfway to the beach from our rented apartment—I hear the inevitable "Mommy? I actually really do have to go to the bathroom. Really bad."

I did that bit of choreography then known as The Irritated Mom Shuffle: grab kid by the head, do an acute 180-degree turn with large quantities of stuff swinging around in your wake, and then commence frog marching the kid in the other direction.

I probably also grumbled some annoyed oaths under my breath that kind of sounded like "I knew it," and "I told you so," and maybe something close to "dammit." Not necessarily in that order.

"Mommy," he said. "You are forgetting that we have all the time that we need."

And there it was . . . that phrase so often repeated in the children's worship liturgy[1] that my kids frequently repeat it back to me when I am in a fit of frustration over their slowness, or my own inability to get everybody together and out the door with all their stuff intact for the day.

We have all the time that we need. It is a children's mantra so powerful I often repeat it in adult worship; we even crafted an entire Lent sermon series one year out of that very concept. And yet, I need these constant reminders from my kids to pull me out of my annoyance, my feelings of ineptitude, and the frantic pace of this life I've cultivated. Or have I let it cultivate me? Sometimes I wonder.

On the day of this particular reminder, we were spending a few days in our favorite California beach town to "recover" from the previous few days at Disneyland.

To be clear, we are not theme park people. We are National Park people.

We are beach people. We are long-road-trip-to-visit-friends people. We are mountain people. But we are not Mouse people, princess people, or long line people. Until this trip, my kids (then 5 and 7) had never been on an amusement park ride.

So it's a mystery to me why I was suddenly overcome with the overwhelming urge to take my kids to Disneyland. I think I felt some magic window closing. I know that older kids still get excited, and still have fun. But there is an age at which they move past the capacity for a certain kind of little kid joy; when they become more difficult to impress. No longer utterly "wowed" by the fireworks, no longer impressed or moved to gleeful squeals to see their favorite character pass by. Let's face it, there is a moment at which that character becomes a creepy dude in a cowboy suit, a sorority girl in a tiara. And I knew that moment was coming—with every growth spurt, every new surge in vocabulary, every glimpse of their emerging independence, I could see it coming.

I am not one to weep and wail about how fast they grow, or say, "Why can't they just stay little?" or "You've got to enjoy every moment!" In every one of those sentiments I hear a gentle shaming, and a crushing scarcity of time. Of course I don't want them to stay little forever. I refuse to be sad that they are getting bigger, smarter, and more self-sufficient, as nature and the good Lord intended.

But in recognition of that quickly closing window, I still felt the need to go to Disneyland.

So that's how we found ourselves queuing up with 40,000 of our closest friends—to fight through 30-minute lines for 30-second rides. To pay $20 for a sandwich. To touch unspeakably germy surfaces and endure the tantrums of other people's children.

But no, really, it was magical.

It was worth the trip to see their faces lit up under the fireworks, to watch them straining on tiptoe to see the parade go by, and to experience Radiator Springs *in real life*. My little boy could not believe he got to *drive* that race car, and that we *won*. A lifelong Route 66 nerd myself, I may have enjoyed that part just as much as he did.

But even the racing roadsters were not enough to stop the racing mind that keeps company with me the rest of the time. If anything, a crowded theme park invites its own kind of mental chaos. *If we don't get in line for this ride soon . . . If we don't hurry we'll miss . . . How much do we have to get "done" today to make the ticket price worthwhile?* As a writer, my mind was constantly racing with blog posts: Disney and white privilege; Disney and extreme gender typing; Disney and the heteronormative world (in spite of their gay-friendly work policies); Disney and body image; Disney and the narrative of American excess.

No, I kept telling myself. *I'm on vacation.*

Do you know the Croc, who swallowed the clock and now follows Captain Hook around everywhere? I see her in a whole new light now.

The whole point of vacation is to escape that ticking clock. Whether it's the ticking time clock of the workday, or the constant reminders that children are growing up quickly, vacation is an invitation to be in the moment in a way that we don't often allow ourselves—especially if we are parents, or any kind of working professional managing a daily rotation of demands on our time and energy and mental territory.

For some people, Disneyland may be a perfectly okay place to find that alternate rhythm, that off-the-clock status. But for me, it was not that. Which is why Sunday of vacation week found me at the beach. As I watched the waves roll in, enjoying a rare moment to myself, the coastal Episcopalians tried to lure me to worship with lovely chimes. But even that I heard as another *tick-tick-tick* . . . a subtle demand on my time and space. An alarm that "something is starting, something is happening somewhere, and if you don't hurry you will miss it."

I ignored the invitation and instead matched my breath to the liturgy of waves. In that rise and fall I heard (again) the reminder that God's rhythms are holy, and that they don't look like calendar blocks or ticking clocks. They roll like tides and turn like seasons. They move like kids growing exactly as they are supposed to. And sometimes they even rest.

From the beach that morning, I wandered to a used bookstore—my other church home—and meandered through rows of new releases, vintage genre paperbacks, and the original (original!) works of Byron. In that backwards evolution of words, I heard not a scarcity of time, but the fullness of it. Stories and poetry and history, folded neatly into those shelves. Our life in words, somehow whole and bound and processed for retail. The fullness of it all washed over me like a baptism.

I located the owner and asked him if they might have a Western Americana section. "Well," he said. "Have you got all day?"

"You know what? I actually kind of do," I said.

Privilege check. To take a vacation—even if this particular kind of trip was a big splurge for my family—is a big luxury that the majority of the world experiences rarely, if ever.

Everyone I know feels crunched for time. They work hard. Outside of work, their other time is filled with kids' activities, a social life, and the demands of caring for home and property. These are all points of privilege. From the rush of the kids' soccer or dance schedule to the beckoning yard work, home repairs, and weekend gatherings to which we promised to bring a side and a dessert, all of these things are part of the fullness of life, and they are gifts.

But sometimes the fullness can leave us empty.

Americans let an estimated 658 million vacation days go unused last year.[2] Or, to take another angle, nearly half of Americans had unused vacation time at the end of the year; about one fourth of American workers don't get paid time off at all. Not even holidays.[3] Any way you shake it—we are exhausted. We don't know how to step away from these full and busy lives that we've cultivated, and it takes a toll on us—physically and spiritually. And we don't know how to be together with our people without plans—and it takes a toll on the depth of our relationships.

Our pace is hard on our human connections, and also brutal on the environment. We are constantly rushing to work harder so that we can have more stuff. We spend fuel in getting there, and then the manufacturers have to keep up with the pace of all that stuff we "need." And then we fill all of our scant free time taking care of that stuff. It's a vicious cycle.

Whether we are middle- to upper-class or working-class Americans, our pace and work ethic affect that of those who work with and for us. Like it or not, we live in a "trickle down" economy. Some would have us believe that is a good thing— that success for those at the top means as much for those at the so-called bottom of the food chain. We who live in states that have experimented with this sort of model—namely, Kansas— know this not to be true. At least, it is not true in monetary terms.

It is true, however, in deeper, more human ways. What happens "upstream" affects those "downstream." Thus claims the great wisdom of Wendell Berry, in his version of the golden rule. Much of Berry's work explores the complicated relationship between people and land. His collection *Home Economics,* in particular, explores the often dehumanizing effect of the world's system of goods and services. Berry questions the system in which we live—the one that wants to squeeze as much productivity out of the land and its people without considering the well-being of either, without acknowledging the lasting effects of our hurried shortsightedness, and without looking at the wholeness of people and communities. To this end, he employs the term "The Great Economy" as another way of understanding the kingdom of God.[4]

After all, there is so much more to a person than tangible net worth: the ability to care for the earth, the work of being a good neighbor, and the raising and nurture of children. Farming, giving life, and living in community; these are critical to an economy that does not operate on a dollar system.

The mandate to rest and restore is perhaps God's greatest gift to us. It is an invitation to remember and live into a holy purpose. In all its beautiful and life-giving simplicity, Sabbath-keeping is not just for our own good; it is a value that, when practiced faithfully, can transform the world.

The greater the demands and expectations of our shared human economy, the harder and more destructive the pace becomes for those in every layer of that working system. It means the disappearing middle class is afraid to take a day off and the working class couldn't take a day off if they wanted to. Many American families fall into the category of "working poor." They work full time, often in multiple jobs, but can barely make ends meet, and do not qualify for benefits like healthcare, retirement, and certainly not paid time off. This growing demographic of workers is directly impacted by the increasing demand for unlimited amounts of stuff at a low cost.

We've created and enabled an economy in which people are consumed—literally and figuratively—with keeping up an excessive and consumptive way of life.

Enough.

Since travel is out of reach for such a vast segment of the population, a vacation is obviously not the answer. However, the rhythm that we find when we get out of town—away from e-mail, phone, piles of paperwork, and the ticking timeclock that we punch, in one way or another, each day—that rhythm is the way of salvation. And whether or not we manage to get out of town for an actual vacation once a year, that rhythm is one that we need to find (and keep) in regular and disciplined ways. Our spirit, our family, our community, and our planet all depend on it.

As with so many social and cultural ills of our time, it is one thing entirely to name and critique the broken places. People of God are called not just to lament the sickness, but also to articulate and model a better way. For those of us with the privilege of freedom to take paid time off, work flexible hours when our family needs demand it, and even get out of town for a few days every year (even if we feel, much of the time, that we are barely getting the bills paid), it is even more critical that we learn to root our daily lives and our relationships in that Sabbath kind of breath. Our communities will be better for it. And we might, in some small way, even begin to reshape the local economy that can be so hard on those in the most vulnerable economic positions.

People are not things to be consumed. Consciously, we know this to be true at every layer of the economy, from the 1 percent to the working poor to the developing world. But if we want to see that truth lived out in the world around us, that holy knowing must be rooted in a kind of rest and belonging that we too often have forgotten how to claim.

PRACTICING SABBATH AT HOME

The week at the beach—or camping in the mountains or visiting Grandma—all of that stepping away from the ticking clock is really just practice. It is a reminder to find the Sabbath rhythm at least once a week, in smaller ways, at home. Finding time to just be with our friends, family, and neighbors in unplanned and unhurried ways. To breathe. To enjoy the home as sacred space that is cultivated in love—whether that home is a one-bedroom apartment in the city or a house in a sprawling suburb, or something in between. That space—and the stuff in it—is a sanctuary.

When my children say to me, "We have all the time that we need," it always forces me out of whatever rush I'm in, and into a more quietly intentional place. What demands on my time have led me to be abrupt (or even hostile) towards my kids' slower pace or their needs? How many of those demands are self-imposed? And what am I missing in the space between?

It is difficult—between kids' schedules, my husband and I piecing together work and childcare, and the pace of life at a busy church—to always carve out a single day of the week in which everyone is at home, together, and being relatively still. So I have come to think of Sabbath as a certain pace, mental state, and level of energy—one that can be obtained, if not for a whole week at a time, or even a whole day every week—for at least a part of every day.

And this has made all the difference.

In the summer, maybe that looks like an hour of enforced reading time on the couch. Or an evening sitting on the back porch with a glass of wine for the grown-ups and a glass jar for catching lightning bugs for the kids.

In the fall, maybe that is making sure we have at least two Saturdays of the month where the calendar doesn't get absorbed with activities, so we can enjoy a day of front yard leaf jumping, or a day trip to the Flint Hills to enjoy the fall color.

Maybe, in any season, it is what I call "the discipline of dinnertime": making the effort to get everyone to the table at the same time, even if we are just having leftovers, and even if it is squeezed between activities. I'll confess that sometimes, when my husband is working late and I've had a busy week and the kids are wild, I like to feed them first. Then I wait until they go to bed, heat up an assortment of Trader Joe's frozen appetizers, and settle in with Netflix and a box of wine. That is pure heaven sometimes. And I guess that is its own kind of Sabbath.

But true Sabbath is not just rest. It is a restful being together—and getting to the table at the same time is one way of claiming that space.

Another thing that can happen, when we let ourselves get caught up in the frantic getting of stuff and doing of things, is that we lose touch with our neighbors. Sometimes our best friends. And maybe even the people who live in our own home. So maybe Sabbath involves a certain releasing of expectations when it comes to entertaining. Sometimes an impromptu neighborhood cookout or a last-minute potluck with good friends—dust in the corners and all—is just what our spirits need to slow down a bit.

In many cases, it is what our marriages need as well. It is no wonder, with the pace that many of our families keep just to get by, that those connections become fragile. It is no wonder that the divorce rate, though down from the past decade or so, is still a testament to how many challenges the modern union faces on a daily basis. Without placing shame or judgment on those whose unions have ended in divorce, I wonder how much healthier our marriages could be if we adopted this discipline of Sabbath time as a family unit, and held accountable the other people in our homes when that discipline is broken. I wonder how much closer we could feel to our spouses if every spare moment we had together was not so often absorbed with the logistics of managing a household. And all of its stuff.

Sabbath is not just rest. It is people. It is getting out of the rut of our stuff and our work and even the weight of our past hurts and disappointments, and opening ourselves up to connection. We don't have to be great gurus or practitioners of a certain faith to enact this kind of restorative Sabbath vibe on the world.

However you practice Sabbath at home, the key is resisting the urge to worship, as Barbara Brown Taylor says, at "the altar of busyness."[5] Whether that means limiting kids' activities to a one-per-season standard (which is what we try to do), or learning to keep excess stuff from swallowing us whole, or just learning to say no to the things that will push our schedules from full to full-on meltdown, what it means for us may not be what it means for you. But the goal is that we learn the holy rhythms that fill and renew us for the work at hand. And in the meantime, that will keep our spirits growing in the way of the sacred.

PRACTICING SABBATH IN COMMUNITY

Irony: When the desire to answer God's call to Sabbath is rooted in faith, and yet the church is often one of the obstacles to practicing that rhythm faithfully.

This is not just because I'm a pastor and church is my job. Being a part of an active faith community is often one of the things that make people feel "busy," in a way that makes it hard to rest. Even on the weekends.

The church is a busy place. A thriving church, even more so. There are events and activities, service opportunities and worship, not to mention the call to gather in various settings throughout the week/month/year. All of these things might be good, even life-giving; but the faith community often struggles to balance that healthy pace—one that perpetuates growth and engagement—with the restful rhythm that we so desperately need, in response to our otherwise saturated lives.

As an extrovert who is *all about the activities;* and a vocational minister, who relishes all of these doings as signs of life and growth in my congregation; I am still learning how to put Sabbath into practice in the life of the church.

One way of doing that is to address the sheer volume of meetings that we have on the calendar at any given moment. Have mercy. Church folk do love meetings. And while meetings are important for the planning and doing of the Lord's work—perhaps they are not as important as we sometimes make them.

I once heard of a church that canceled all of its meetings in the season of Lent. If a group did get together during that season, they used the time for prayer and study of Scripture. I was in awe of the transformative potential of this practice. And it doesn't have to be in Lent. Maybe for your church it works better in Advent, leading up to the holidays. Or maybe in summer, when people pretty much don't show up for stuff anyway. Pick one—but every faith community can find a way to reset its internal clock. Using that span of time to remember that

the call of the church is not just to rush through cycles of epic programming: *VBS! Fall youth kickoff! ALL THE CHRISTMAS THINGS! Lenten study! Summer service trips!*
It is always time for something.
Sometimes that schedule feels like success. And certainly there is some connection to the level of activity and the health of the congregation. But congregations can also fall victim to the sort of economy that leads to burnout. In this economy, there is always stuff "happening." But good leaders start to say "no" to taking on leadership positions; worship attendance becomes sporadic; engagement wanes; and church becomes just one more thing to add to the calendar.

I don't have the secret to helping a community find that balance between full and busy. But I do know that, sometimes, it is okay to just be God's people. Together in prayer without an agenda. Together in worship, without the press of a capital campaign, a big event, or an impending set of deadlines. If we set our intentions as community toward this kind of togetherness, and model it in the life of faith that we share, it will be far easier for our families to claim it in their own ways, in their own time and space.

SABBATH IN SCRIPTURE

If the biblical story begins in abundance, it also begins with a deep and abiding trust in that abundance. When God rests on the seventh day, it is an expectation set for the rest of us. We can't be faithful caretakers of creation if we are always run ragged. Nothing is lost if we rest, and, in fact, the health of creation depends upon our resting.

Throughout the Old Testament, there are practices, even several books full of laws, that model and insist upon the need for rest—down to the practice of letting the fields rest every seventh year.

Even the earth needs a break. It is not just here to be consumed.

My favorite Scripture on Sabbath is from the Gospel of
Matthew; more specifically, from Eugene Peterson's modern
interpretation of Jesus' words in *The Message:*

> "Are you tired? Worn out? Burned out on religion? Come
> to me. Get away with me and you'll recover your life. I'll
> show you how to take a real rest. Walk with me and work
> with me—watch how I do it. Learn the unforced rhythms of
> grace. I won't lay anything heavy or ill-fitting on you. Keep
> company with me and you'll learn to live freely and lightly."
> Matt. 11:28–30

In more traditional translations, this is where we find the
bit about "come unto me/all ye who labor/his yoke is easy/
his burden is light." All the makings of a soaring aria from
Handel's *Messiah.* But I'm partial to the Peterson version, primarily because of that thing about "the unforced rhythms of
grace." That may be the loveliest and truest invitation in all of
Scripture, and one that speaks to the depths of my soul when
I am deeply tired.

Imagine how that invitation would resonate with the truly
weary; the ones doing heavy emotional labor, like caring for
a sick loved one or counseling trauma victims. The ones who
work two or three jobs just to feed their family, and still struggle
with food and housing insecurity. The ones who labor under
the culture of excess toward which we contribute every day.
Part of our calling as Sabbath keepers, in fact, is to be mindful
of all those who "labor," and to work for justice in extending
sacred rest to all people.

The unforced rhythms of grace: It is not just a call into
recovered life, but a call to lay down our own stuff—or our
own expectations of stuff—and follow a Jesus way of life. One
that is full without being busy.

The Psalms are full of the praise of creation and the spirit of
Sabbath restoration. One of my favorites is Psalm 8.

> O LORD, our Sovereign,
>   how majestic is your name in all the earth!

You have set your glory above the heavens.
  Out of the mouths of babes and infants
you have founded a bulwark because of your foes,
  to silence the enemy and the avenger.
When I look at your heavens, the work of your fingers,
  the moon and the stars that you have established;
what are human beings that you are mindful of them,
  mortals that you care for them?
Yet you have made them a little lower than God,
  and crowned them with glory and honor.
You have given them dominion over the works of your
    hands;
  you have put all things under their feet,
all sheep and oxen,
  and also the beasts of the field,
the birds of the air, and the fish of the sea,
  whatever passes along the paths of the seas.
O LORD, our Sovereign,
  how majestic is your name in all the earth!

Nothing will stoke your sense of wanderlust and prime you for a summer of road-tripping adventure like Ken Burns' documentary *National Parks: America's Best Idea*. It is part history, part storytelling, and part liturgy—an invitation to dwell in the wonder of creation for a while, and remember, with awestruck humility, that these places were created for our pleasure. We are called to venture out into it from time to time; both to take in the beauty of it, and also to be reminded of our collective call to care for it.

When I say it is part liturgy, I'm not exaggerating. The first installment of the miniseries is actually titled "The Scripture of Nature." In it, a park ranger comments that, in these places, we "don't have to be reminded to worship." The earth beneath your feet is a sanctuary; the sky above and vistas around speak to the power of the creator. It is church, in other words. Church without the name tags, the bulletins, and the Styrofoam coffee cups.

It is not easy to get to places like the Grand Tetons, Yosemite, and Zion. They are not right off the interstate, not a

10-minute shuttle ride from a major airport, and there is not a chain motel or a drive-thru burger in sight—you have to really *want* to get there. Which is kind of the point. We go because not everything should be convenient. We go because, sometimes, we just need to feel small.

We need to feel small not in the negative sense of having been demeaned or talked down to but in the cosmic sense. We need to feel small in a way that fills, inspires, and uplifts us; we need to feel small in a way that reminds us of our place in the broad story of creation. It is a small part; it is a critical part.

That small but important place is exactly where the psalmist is standing when he writes, "What are humans, that you are mindful of them?"

When you think about it, all of our deep human restlessness stems from this same question. The Psalmist wants to know why the God of all creation would bother to notice us. Or if you want to be all Monty Python about it: "What is the meaning of life?" Or, more to the point, the age-old question posed by Wendell Berry: "What are people for?" In these human questions, we hear echoes of the psalmist. It's a call not just to acknowledge the dehumanizing effect that our industry has on the world but also to actively push against that cycle. To participate in the work of "re-humanizing" the lived experience.

We might also call that the kingdom of God.

There are two divergent world economies: one that reduces people to their earning and output potential, and one that takes in the whole person. But it seems those two economies hold a truth in common, after all: you get out what you invest. Nurture the earth, and it will produce fruit to feed us; treat people like people, and they will express that embodied humanity right back to us—in good and life-giving ways.

This care of the earth and other is written into our origin story—it's right there in the first pages of Genesis, the first spoken word of creation. It is our primary calling as God's people and citizens of the world. And when we are tired, it's worth remembering that this is who we are created to be. We are stewards of all that lies beneath our feet. We are worshipers under the altar of all that cosmic grandeur overhead. It is OK to rest. It is OK to be still, and to breathe. Savor the smallness of the good and basic life plan that is woven into all of creation, if we will stop and hear it once in a while. If we believe in a God who created us in the image of holiness, to be a living embodiment of the sacred; if we claim to follow Jesus, who lived so that we may know life; then we know we are so much more than what we produce, and what we can prosper.

What are people for? What are humans, that God is mindful of them? We are here. We are here, rooted to our place between the earth and the sky; dirt under our feet, and all the mystery of the universe, spinning overhead. We are here, putting into the world what we hope to see it produce.

We are here, and we are a part of it all. Sometimes, that is all we have to be. And isn't that good news?

AROUND THE TABLE:
QUESTIONS FOR DISCUSSION

1. What are the biggest challenges to finding Sabbath time with your family? Are the challenges internal or external?
2. Think of a moment when you felt truly and deeply rested. Where were you? What were you doing, or not doing? How might you be able to find that same rhythm in a more daily fashion?
3. What positive effects might a different pace of life have on your community and the environment?
4. Does your faith community have any shared Sabbath practices? What are they? Or if not, how might you carve some into your liturgical calendar?

4

Nonviolence: Beyond Turning the Other Cheek

We are tired of lighting candles and singing sad songs. We are tired of "praying for peace" and "sending our condolences." We are tired of shielding our children from the evening news. We are tired of writing endless letters to representatives and receiving form letter responses that read something like this, "We hear your concerns, and we remain committed to protecting the Second Amendment. . . ."

We are tired of words and we are tired of carnage. We are tired of sifting through the hymnal, the liturgy, and the Bible for the theme "response to violence."

These are conversations we have at my church every time there is another horrific shooting or terror attack on the news. Which is, let's face it, often. Daily, it seems. I'm starting to feel like these services need to be built into the liturgical calendar in more specific ways. Like, *Candlelight Service for a Mass Shooting during Advent; Litany for a Terror Attack during Lent; A Pentecost Prayer to End Gun Violence.* Surely those are differently nuanced situations. Or how about *Prayer Service for a Mass Shooting Elsewhere* vs. *Prayer and Comfort When the Mass Shooting Is in Your Own Community?* Are those different things? Or how about *Weekly Prayer of Contrition for the Daily Loss of Life We Have Come to Accept as Part of Our Culture?*

Enough. We are tired of singing sad songs.

Of course, statistics tell us that the world is actually getting *less* violent, not more so. The 24-hour news cycle and our hyper-connected planet simply draw more attention to violence, exposing us to horrific acts in parts of the globe that might, a century ago, have felt a world away. That is the gift and the burden of the digital age: we are suddenly aware of the full scale of human atrocity and we move with a growing awareness that we are all connected. Regardless of how much "better" the violence is than it was in centuries past, the fact remains that we live in a violent world.

Recently, while working on one of many sermons about "peace," I found myself alternating between the language of "peace" and "nonviolence." I noticed that I was using these terms interchangeably.

When you're a writer or a preacher (or both) you are always looking for artfully nuanced ways to restate what you've already said. Ways to reinforce for impact without being redundant. (See what I did there?) It's nothing new for me to use multiple expressions to cover the same topical ground. But in this case, it gave me pause. Peace and nonviolence are not the same thing. They might be two parts of the same whole, but they are different entities.

The problem was, I didn't exactly understand how.

So I took a minute. I had an intense internal discussion about what is implied by the word "peace" and what is meant by the term "nonviolence."

Peace, in the biblical, global, and/or Hallmark Christmas card sense, is a *state* of being. *Nonviolence*, however, is a *way* of being; a practice, activity, philosophy, or avenue by which peace may be attained.

In other words, if peace is the desired state of being, then nonviolence is an intentional set of practices by which we might arrive there.

The challenge, of course, is learning to not just value peace in the abstract, but to practice nonviolence within the reality of a distinctly violent world and culture. When the Christian narrative itself is rooted in supreme violence—from the cross to the Old Testament notion of an angry, violent God—and then that narrative is reinforced by a culture that delights in violence as entertainment—how do we model a counterculture of nonviolence at home and in our faith communities?

Just as "love," in a broad and un-nuanced sense, can be referenced and then completely overridden by a lack of compassion, so, too, can "peace" be reduced to hollow sentimentality by a failure to practice the way of intentional nonviolence. Just look at the apparent marriage, for example, of the NRA and the Evangelical Christian voter base. Or *The Passion of the Christ,* a popular movie that dwells heavily in the graphic suffering scenes portraying Jesus' crucifixion. The film, and others like it, are an extreme glorification of violence—otherwise known as "torture porn." This movie is simply one more witness to the violent nature of atonement-based theology, favored among many conservative Christians.

The whole idea that God will cast into eternal suffering all those who do not pray the correct prayer of atonement and adopt the appropriate set of beliefs and behaviors thereafter—this in itself is a violent notion. And it's a little absurd to claim, on the one hand, a God of peace and mercy, while also insisting on this violent theodicy. Perhaps it is this very tension that has often placed Christians on the wrong side of history when it comes to speaking against violence.

Also problematic is the notion of substitutionary atonement, in which God's lust for blood must be somehow satisfied, and so Jesus must be sacrificed to save us from paying that price. This theory of atonement "has come to dominate the landscape of Christian faith in America, especially in its more popular expressions," say theologians Joel Green and Mark Baker. "According to this theory, humanity has, in its sin, turned away from God and so merits divine punishment.

Jesus, in his death on the cross, died in place of sinful humanity at God's behest, and in doing so he took upon himself the punishment humanity ought to have suffered."[1] With these threads woven so tightly through our historic understanding of who God is, it's no wonder that people of faith often take part in the world's violent narrative without a second thought.

We reinforce violence in some of the most asinine ways, in the guise of jokes, sound bites, and polite banter. I can think of endless shared cultural norms that are supposed to make us chuckle or nod in approval, but that really empower an acceptance of violence that should be utterly counter to the Christian way of life.

Take, for example, the tired "dad with pretty daughter" shtick. You know, like maybe the pastor makes a joke from the pulpit about fathers who clean their shotguns as young suitors show up at the door. Or maybe you've even seen the T-shirts: "Guns don't kill people. Dads with pretty daughters do." As if the price to pay for being a teenage boy is death. As if I should somehow find that funny, as the mother of a son.

This kind of "Ha, ha, I'll kill you, no not really, I'm joking, but you never know, I might!" humor is problematic, to say the least. It feeds the notion that violence somehow answers our every insecurity, and that weapons are power. It fuels our country's obsession with firearms, and the freedom to carry them anytime, anywhere, whatever the cost to human life. It's not a harmless aside, by any means. It's a troubling line of dialogue.

But even more troubling, and even more contradictory, is continued Christian support for the death penalty. Contemporary people of faith seem to have forgotten the "scandal of the cross,"[2] and the dreadful social and spiritual implications of state-sanctioned, corporate violence.

Kelly Gissendaner was a high-profile death row inmate, convicted in 1998 of enlisting her then-boyfriend to kill her husband. It was a gruesome case—one in which she was ultimately sentenced to death, while the man who actually committed the crime went free. But that's not why the story was widely publicized.

Over the course of seventeen years in prison, Gissendaner found faith. She began courses in theological education and ultimately became a chaplain to her fellow inmates. Because of this fairly dramatic conversion story, Christians everywhere—from the most conservative to the most progressive, and even the pope—called for her pardon. Not her release—just a stay of execution, because she was the very image of what "restorative justice" can and should look like.

On the one hand, they were right—no one should be executed who has clearly experienced a dramatic transformation of faith and humanity; one who embodies the spirit of "reform" on which our prison system claims to be based (but which is so seldom successful). On the other hand, it is fundamentally problematic to say that the reason we should not kill a person is because they've found Jesus.

As Christians, we are for mercy. Not because the criminal has come to know Jesus. But because we already do.

Gissendaner was executed in 2015, in spite of widespread support for a stay of her sentence. But today, nearly 3,000 people remain on America's death row. So this work is far from finished. Kelly Gissendaner's life was one life that might have been saved, because everyone loves a conversion story. But look at the most hardened, heinous, unrepentant criminals in the system. The ones whose crimes keep us up at night. The ones who show no remorse. The ones who did not become chaplains after a cinematic "come to Jesus" moment. For them, assume there is no shred of "worthiness" that might merit sparing their lives.

What, then, about their inherent worth as a child of God? Is that not enough? Is that dim light of createdness, the one that bears the image of the holy, not reason enough to stop this barbaric practice, once and for all?

For many, it is not. For many, criminal justice is about vengeance, above all. Because we've seen too many cowboy movies.

There are also alarming statistics about the number of innocent people on death row. Any one of these truths—the human potential for transformation, the inherent holiness of all humanity, and the high margin of error that accompanies a large and fallible system—would be reason enough to stop the madness that is capital punishment.

But.

Broad support for the death penalty is just one example of how secular American identity has manipulated the Christian narrative; how Christian family "values" have become entangled with a rhetoric, distinctly political and cultural, that doesn't have much to do with the way of Christ.

I've spoken on interfaith panel discussions about violence. And every time, what I hear from my conversation partners is the same: first, a shared commonality between all the major religions of the world and their shared commitment to peace as a core value. And whenever I'm in dialogue with people from other religious backgrounds, I hear the same questions: How can Christians—whose savior proclaimed a radical way of nonviolence, and who was, himself, executed by the state—embrace the cultural norms of violence that are so cancerous to our own society? In everything from gun culture to the death penalty to the programming we watch on TV?

I never have a good answer. "I know," is all I can say. "We are working on it."

Theologian Walter Wink explores the ways in which Jesus teaches not just the principles of nonviolence, but "The Third Way."[3] The Third Way moves beyond passive resistance to creative ways of asserting authority. For instance, to "turn the other cheek"—a biblical directive interpreted by many as allowing someone to hit you again—is really to rob the oppressor of the power to publicly humiliate you.

In the same way, Jesus instructs that if someone robs you of your coat, you should give them your cloak as well. That directive is rejected out-of-hand in a culture that values capitalism and retributive justice. But when we dismiss Jesus' words as somehow passé or not relevant to our time, we miss some nuanced layers that could be deeply transformative in our own time and place. Wink roots his "Third Way" in the Greek word *antistenai*. In English translations, that word is usually interpreted as weakness. But beyond that surface meaning, it can also be understood as "to set against." To creatively turn the tables in a way that removes the oppressor's power without doing physical harm; that empowers the oppressed without the need for bloodshed or force.

If a person has robbed you of your clothing—well, clearly, you would be naked. In the ancient world of Jesus' ministry setting, the shame of nakedness *is not on the person who is naked, but on the one who SEES the nakedness.* (Think of Noah's son Ham, cursed for laying eyes on his drunk, naked father.) So, if you were to strip off your remaining undergarments and hand them over to a thief in a public square—it's a pretty funny way to really turn things around on the person who thinks they have power over you. Even though it sounds like a Bugs Bunny cartoon that involves someone wearing a barrel over their naked selves, this is actually an act of prophetic defiance. And one of many ways that, in this new understanding of "setting against," transforms potential violence to potential restoration.

I remember hearing a story on the radio about Julio Diaz, a young social worker from the Bronx. One night, as he stepped off the train and headed to his usual neighborhood diner, he was approached by a young man with a knife.

Diaz quickly handed over his wallet before things could escalate. But as the teenage boy turned to leave, Diaz said, "Hey, wait a minute. You forgot something. If you're going to be robbing people for the rest of the night, you might as well take my coat to keep you warm."

This is starting to sound like a parable.

Diaz went on to say, "If you're willing to risk your freedom for a few dollars, then I guess you must really need the money. I mean, all I wanted to do was get dinner and if you really want to join me . . . hey, you're more than welcome."

The two went to the diner and sat in Diaz' usual booth. Over the course of their meal, the kid was in awe at how many people stopped by to say hello. Everyone from the dishwasher to the manager seemed to know his host. The young man eventually asked Diaz if he owned the place.

"No, I just eat here a lot," was the reply.

"But . . . you're even nice to the dishwasher," said his guest, still in disbelief.

"Well, haven't you been taught you should be nice to everybody?"

"Yeah. But I didn't think people actually behaved that way," said the would-be thief.

That point of exchange alone would make this a story of dramatic transformation. But one more turn makes this a living example of how the "Third Way" can creatively turn a violent situation into a moment of resurrection.

Because when it was time to pay, Diaz told the kid, "Look, I guess you're going to have to pay for this bill . . . because you have my money and I can't pay for this. But if you give me my wallet back, I'll gladly treat you."

The kid handed over the wallet without missing a beat. Diaz gave him $20 . . . and asked for the kid's knife in return.

The young man handed over his weapon, and then went on his way.[4]

In a world of stand-your-ground laws, where Mr. Diaz would have been perfectly entitled to shoot this young man and would probably not have suffered consequences, this response is an extraordinary display of the intentional way of nonviolence.

If we are starting a club for people who effectively model the "Third Way" of Jesus, then Antoinette Tuff is another member who needs to line up and be counted. A few years ago, Tuff averted a school shooting by talking down the gunman.

You have heard it said, *the only thing that can stop a bad guy with a gun is a good guy with a gun.* But verily, I say unto you, that this woman is a total badass . . . and her only weapons were prayer, courage, and compassion. Verily I say unto you: the world is violent, but there is always another way.

Tuff saved the lives of countless children when a gunman entered the school where she works; she engaged him with a clear head, a calm voice, and a kindness that ultimately led him to surrender. That, friends, is what happens when faith meets courage and steps into the void.

"I just started praying for him," she said. "I just started talking to him . . . and let him know what was going on with me and that it would be OK . . . I give it all to God, I'm not the hero. I was terrified."[5]

Terrified or not, Tuff was tough . . . in every way except for physically. And while I don't doubt that she would have put her body between the gunman and innocent children, it did not come to that. She was willing to make herself vulnerable in another way, perhaps in a Third Way. She shared some of her own painful life experiences. She connected with this man who was obviously hurting in a way that few of us can even imagine. She prayed. She made herself fully present to the pain of another person. She transformed a horrific situation into a day without a death toll; a day without another prayer service of sad songs and lighted candles. And her story is inspiring many people to think more deeply about what it means to live the faith, calling it up in a moment's notice when another person is in need. Any person at all.

All that, and she didn't even have a gun.

I don't pretend that every other tragic, mass shooting might have been averted *if only* a faithful, godly woman had been on hand to pray the bad guys away. In fact, I'm sure there were many faithful people, in each of those situations, who acted out of love and mercy—even if the outcome was drastically different. I'm also not saying that nobody should use force, ever, to stop someone from harming innocent children. But on this one occasion at least, love was louder than baser instincts, more effective than legislation or constitutional rights, and far more powerful than the language of violence that permeates so much of our communal life.

Here's how we know that Antoinette's way was the Jesus way . . . because even if we can't count the lives of all the children she saved, we can count one life for certain: she saved the gunman. Who does that? Not most people. Not in our warped secular understanding of justice. But in God's story, even the bad guy hears the still, small voice of mercy, and is transformed.

The right to bear arms is important to our national identity, and to personal freedom. I know that beating all our swords into plowshares is not really a viable option in our current climate. So keep the guns and the Second Amendment. But remember this: when our founding fathers penned the Constitution, they had no idea that "arms" would get so big, so powerful, and so plentiful. They never imagined that the tools used for hunting and necessary defense would so quickly evolve into legally sanctioned weapons of mass destruction.

But Jesus did.

And that's why Jesus cautions us that God's kind of justice does not look like ours. He reminds us that, in the face of a hopeless situation—even when violence feels like the only answer—there is almost always another way.

The other way is never easy, it is never popular, and it may not always make sense alongside the fearful narrative in which we live. It would rarely make a good movie (except in the case of Antoinette Tuff. I'd like to see that movie). But every now and then, an Antoinette or a Julio comes along to remind us of God's way . . . and of the better story that we are called to live. We may always live in tension between the world's brand of good news and the Jesus kind. The world's kind says violence can only be stopped by more violence; but Jesus and Antoinette know a better way.

I don't have an easy answer about finding that balance between maintaining personal freedom and remaining faithful to the Jesus way of peace. Living faithfully in that tension involves a level of complex conversation and soul searching that defies nearly every element of popular culture. But if a few faithful people can stand in the void between chaos and grace, and somehow be the presence of God in an impossible situation, then surely we Jesus people can find ways to challenge the violent nature of the world in which we live.

When we seek to walk faithfully in the way of Jesus, then Jesus shows up in the flesh—in people who are brave enough to tell a better story. Their way is still there for us if we can find it and follow. And the darkness has not overcome it.

One of my goals as a parent and as a pastor is to so thoroughly teach peace and nonviolence—as both a state of desired being and a practical way of life—that our children and the members of our community are hardwired to respond to the violence of the world in just this way. Nothing could be more life-giving, more transformative, or more true to the living gospel of Jesus Christ as effectively modeling this posture for our children and our faith communities.

PRACTICING NONVIOLENCE AT HOME

My kids love the movie *Peter Pan*. The old-school Disney one. And after experiencing the ride at Disneyland, my son was particularly obsessed. There was talk of Peter Pan birthday parties, Peter Pan Halloween costumes, Peter Pan movie night (again!)—so I thought, why not read the book?

Because it's violent and awful, that's why! I was an English major, so I knew, in some part of my brain, that Victorian children's literature can get a little dark. But geez. Every other paragraph I was having to subtly edit stuff about wars with the "redskins," not to mention the routine killing of pirates, for sport. About three-quarters of the way through, I gave it up like a bad job and now we are reading *Ramona* instead. My inner 8-year-old is ecstatic.

Many child health experts estimate that the average American child will witness thousands of murders on television before turning 18. You may assume that is negligent parenting, but the older I get, the more I'm starting to see how it can happen, best intentions aside. Not long ago we were watching *Finding Nemo* when it aired on television. We were not expecting blood and guts and horror during the commercials, but we were wrong. At every break, they were promoting new shows for a 20-something audience. I can only describe the genre as dramedy-horror. There were people screaming, people chasing other people, and at one point, an actual dead body hanging from the ceiling.

Did I mention this was at the commercial break for *Finding Nemo?* On a Sunday afternoon? How did some board of execs, somewhere, not put together that perhaps children would be watching at that moment?

Let me pause to recognize that this is the ultimate first-world concern—that the commercial breaks during our children's entertainment are not appropriate for children. I can make this kind of violence disappear with a click of the remote, while for many children in the world, it is a daily reality. But if television is going to be a part of our first-world lives, then we have to take part in discerning what images and ideas they're exposed to, while also acknowledging the ways in which violent image becomes violent reality.

If even the stuff we have deemed kid-friendly viewing comes with this kind of bloodshed, it is worth saying something to the people who decide these things. Not just for my own kids, but for everyone else's kids too. So I went to the network's website and emailed them. Then, I went to their Facebook page—and found that the parents of America were lighting them up with similar comments of outrage:

"Thanks, guys, I just had to explain to my 5-year-old what a hooker is."

"Seriously? Dead bodies hanging from the ceiling during a Disney Movie??"

"Hey people, my toddler is not your target demographic for that murder show. What were you thinking?"

It felt like going to church, actually, reading all those comments. Smart, thoughtful people gathered (even if virtually) for a purpose. Mostly, I was heartened to see that so many people do still care what their kids are exposed to on TV and elsewhere. Some days I feel like we have given up trying to protect that part of childhood innocence, and just figure they're all going to see the blood and guts eventually. Why fight it?

Because that kind of violence is not an acceptable way of life, for most of us. And I catch hopeful glimpses, every now and then, of how many families truly are trying to reject that blood-and-guts narrative as the inevitable future their children will inherit. But it doesn't come easy. It has to be intentional.

When I read the sheer volume of antiviolence sentiment on that network's public Facebook profile, I thought, "Imagine what we could do together if all these parents got just as riled up about gun control, or anti-bullying movements!"

I grew up in Kentucky, in a small town where just about every household had a gun, mine included. People hunt, people shoot for sport, people have handguns "for protection." I've never been a "take all the guns" kind of advocate. Not only would that never work in a democracy; I don't think it's the answer.

But I will advocate, until the day I die, for stricter regulation—closing the loopholes on background checks; keeping guns out of the hands of violent criminals, the mentally ill, and those suspected of extremist affiliations. And most importantly—I advocate for removing those military-style assault rifles from the public at large.

It's not just because of the statistics, staggering though they are. It's not just because I want to protect my children—and yours—from the possibility of a mass-casualty shooting at their school or elsewhere, though that is also a powerful motivator. It is, ultimately, an expression of faith. Those who claim to follow in the way of Jesus are called to seek the "Third Way," the nonviolent way, in all aspects of life. In the way of Christ—the way that asks us to lay down burdens, give up possessions, and cast off any other number of things that tie us down—there is no room in that life for a weapon designed to take down hundreds of people in a matter of seconds.

The weapons piece, however, is part of a larger whole. A nonviolent home has many elements. What it looks like for me might not be what it looks like for you, but here are a few other ways we practice nonviolence in our home:

Entertainment. What our children watch, and what games they play, will become a part of their view of the world. And a screen world full of police shootings, secret agent bombings, and dead hookers (thanks, family programming folks) will have implications for their adult narratives. It may not be possible to completely shield them from those kinds of images. But that doesn't mean we don't try.

Language. Not just what they hear on TV, but around the house. I worry less about curse words and more about subtle nuances; like casually saying "killing it" or "murdered it" instead of "good job."

No hitting. That means that any hitting of siblings is unacceptable. It also means no spanking. As a method of teaching expected behavior, corporal punishment is ineffective and, as a child psychologist friend of mine says, "a little barbaric." There is a certain hypocrisy present, too, in telling a child "hitting is not OK," and then turning around and whacking them when they step out of line. If we want our values to be more than just things we say sometimes, we will learn to model the way of life of which we speak.

Learn history together. So much history that children come upon in school, and even in church, is of the revisionist variety. It is a "whitewashed" interpretation of the spread of Christianity through colonialism, the founding of our country, westward expansion, slavery, and many points between. In the same way I catch myself editing what my kids read and watch to shield them from unnecessary violence, the stories we tell about our past have been similarly purged of bloodshed. In these cases, however, the edits are dangerous. They put us at risk of repeating history. It is important for people of all ages to learn history that ultimately acknowledges the terrors of war and the atrocities of generations past, so that we learn and evolve as a people. As a family, you can talk about the ways in which these historical movements were justified by leaders at the time; where similar events might be taking place now; and what better way there might be in our own time and place.

Toys. I am that mom. *Guns are not toys.* I don't have a fit if they play with them at other kids' houses. And if they get one as a gift, I let them keep it for a while and then I, shall we say, phase it out. But for the most part, there are no weapons in our house—pretend or otherwise.

Prayers for peace. We are tired of all the prayer vigils. We want an end to violence right now, and "our thoughts and prayers are with the victims' families" rings more hollow than ever. The way of nonviolence is a way of life that is so much more than words, and so much more than a bumper sticker value. But that doesn't mean we can't pray for peace in the meantime. However and whenever your family prays together—whether it is bedtime prayers, dinner grace, or a designated devotional time—there are ways to weave peace and the intentional way of nonviolence into that language of faith you are shaping and living together. Include in your prayers people who live in violent, war-torn places. Ask God to bless the bullies and teach them how to use their words; ask that they might feel loved and safe. Or, simple as it sounds, pray for peace.

PRACTICING NONVIOLENCE IN COMMUNITY

These same practices apply as we live our values in community as well. We don't have to just light candles and mourn every time there's another mass shooting. We can organize to advocate for appropriate weapons regulation. We can peacefully demonstrate when local and state branches of government are in session. We can pray for peace together when it's not even Christmas time. And we can lift up and celebrate stories of people like Tuff and Diaz who have faithfully modeled the way of nonviolence.

While I have never been a bloody Jesus kind of preacher—heavy on sin and salvation and the language of atonement—I also was not really mindful of the many ways that violent theology creeps into other aspects of worship until I came to Saint Andrew, a community that has been deeply intentional (thanks to the leadership of former Associate Pastor Erika) about removing that kind of language and imagery from its liturgy, worship space, and children's ministry.

Systematically removing violence from a church's culture is not easy. The sad news is that I've lost some of my favorite old hymns in this process. Like "Blessed Assurance," and that whole "washed in his blood" thing. We also have to pass on some children's ministry material that is otherwise colorful, fun, and engaging stuff. Curriculum like that often comes with some alarming atonement language not suitable for children. Do we truly want to send our children away from church with images of a battered Jesus, hanging on the cross from the nails in his hands? Some would say yes, that this is an important part of who Jesus is. But on the contrary, placing this image at the heart of our faith story portrays a problematic understanding of who God is—not to mention that it might give a child nightmares for life. This type of imagery also tends to indulge the entertainment value of violence—a cultural reality that we want our churches to push back against, not perpetuate. Quite a bit of mainstream material becomes problematic once you decide to get the blood and guts out of your children's program. Sometimes our minister of faith formation, Denise, just has to write our own stuff. That's more work for her, but ultimately, we wind up with material that is true to who Christ is for us. More importantly, we are helping to shape the narrative for our children as we hope to see it mirrored in the world around us.

NONVIOLENCE IN SCRIPTURE

The first episode of violence in Scripture is the murder of Abel. It is a murder rooted, as mentioned before, in a scarcity mentality . . . there's not enough territory for the both of us, not enough love from our parents, whatever. This posture of "not enough" is the root of much of the world's violence. From our ancient faith narrative to modern-day crimes, from the mugging on the street to global conflict over natural resources, scarcity and bloodshed are inextricably linked.

Following the exile from the garden, the rest of the biblical story is a journey of return. Ask John Milton, or ask any number of biblical scholars who have said the same. The whole of Scripture is the human effort to reclaim "paradise lost," to get back to the garden. Or at least, to that garden state of things: where humans trust in God's provision and want for nothing, and so there is no need for strife or conflict. To that end, many values and practices exhibited in Scripture call for an end to violence as a means of returning to Eden.

Many of the biblical prophets—Isaiah especially—emphasize the principle of *shalom*. *Shalom* is a state beyond objective peace, wherein the community embraces all of creation, together. Lions and lambs lying together. Swords into plowshares. All that good stuff that we have relegated to holiday cards. These were never meant to be just nice ideas that we talk about at the Christmas Eve service. This was God's deep desire for creation, as articulated by prophets ancient and new.

This *shalom* was the faith story of Jesus' upbringing. This was the religious education that shaped him as a child; that he ran away from his parents to teach in the temple; that stirred in him the powerful Sermon on the Mount: "You have heard that it was said, 'An eye for an eye and a tooth for a tooth.' But I say to you, Do not resist an evildoer. But if anyone strikes you on the right cheek, turn the other also; and if anyone wants to sue you and take your coat, give your cloak as well; and if anyone forces you to go one mile, go also the second mile. Give to everyone who begs from you, and do not refuse anyone who wants to borrow from you" (Matt. 5:38–42).

The notion of a "Third Way," radical in Jesus' own time, may sound even more absurd in our own. But it was never supposed to be easy. It was always going to be the lifelong work of faith; a countercultural movement to empower the oppressed, and to bring peace to even the most embattled corners of the earth.

Jesus practiced this way of nonviolence, even to the point of death. Throughout the Gospels, he calls down the powers of heaven to do everything from cast out demons to still a stormy sea—but he does not call down that power to destroy his captors. He rallied the masses everywhere he went—but he did not rally troops to go to war against Pilate and the state.

He died instead. And it turned out to be the most powerful thing that anyone has ever done. Even in his own death, Jesus proclaimed that hope does not lie in any show of human force, but in God's transforming acts of mercy.

The earliest Christians did not have to declare that they were antiviolence. It was simply assumed that if you associated yourself with the teachings of Jesus—who had died at the hands of violent persecutors—then you rejected war, murder, and the use of force to get your way. Over time . . . well, people did what people do. Divergent threads of the Christian narrative emerged. Enter the Crusades, Colonialism, Imperialism, the Pilgrims, and the Ku Klux Klan. Each of these movements claimed some connection to Christianity, but in no way reflect the radical and subversive and intentionally nonviolent teachings of Jesus.

We've been trying to find "another way" ever since.

I know. We are working on it.

AROUND THE TABLE:
QUESTIONS FOR DISCUSSION

1. In what ways has violence become an accepted part of life for you? Is there any level of violence in your theology,

entertainment, or language that feels "appropriate" or "acceptable"?

2. How do you practice nonviolence in your home? In your neighborhood or faith community?
3. What cultural barriers make that practice more difficult?
4. What Scriptures have you heard used out of context to defend capital punishment, "stand your ground" laws, or upholding violent systems in other ways?

5
Joy: Living with Creativity and Purpose

As a parent, there are few joys more complete than watching your children create a bond of their own: watching them play, overhearing them have an actual conversation, witnessing the ways they create their own little world within your world.

I'm proud of my own kids for many reasons, but nothing makes me quite as proud as how close they are and how well they get along (mostly). I try, as often as possible, to be nothing more than a fly on the wall when they are playing together. I may be in the same room, reading or folding laundry, or in the next room, working on dinner or furiously writing a blog post or sermon notes. But I try to stay out of their little world when I can—because that planet is such a miraculous place to me, I don't always want to tread there. It is holy ground.

On one such occasion, I was working on the dishes while they played Legos. They were building their own little world in literal ways. As I listened, I heard them plot what would go where as they carved out a space for every element of life.

"And this will be the school, and here is the post office. This is where the church will be. And here is the liquor store. . . . And then we need a grocery store!"

Hmmm. To intercede or not to intercede?

"Our children are building a Lego liquor store!" I shouted up the stairs. "We are nailing this parenting thing!"

Absolutely nailing it.

As I usually do—if nobody is bleeding or generally being a jerk—I erred on the side of not interceding. It was, in fact, a proud parenting moment for me. Not just because my children understand that the liquor store is one of the fundamental pillars of community life (#motheroftheyear, folks), but because they were, in an unhurried and unplanned moment, learning the art of being together. It was a glimpse of that Sabbath rhythm that we strive for but don't always achieve. They were also, in that moment, being creative—envisioning a world where everything worked and had a purpose; where everything was brightly colored and inviting; and where each of them had a role and a voice in the general order of things.

I'll take it.

Joyful moments like these—with or without the Legos and imaginary booze—can be claimed in the segues, those everyday spaces between holidays, birthday parties and vacations, surprises and big celebrations. Joy is this thing that finds us in the spaces between, even if we are often grasping for it in bigger, more dramatic kinds of expressions.

When I think of joy—some flighty, impulsive creature that flies in on wings and doesn't always stay too long—I remember a particular day in Phoenix, when that thing flew literally above our house, and dropped a gift from the sky.

In a pretty fitting parable for how easy it is to miss that fleeting visitor, I was not home. I'm recalling this episode in third-party memory. But that doesn't make it any less a part of my family's lexicon.

It was one of those rare Phoenix days when everything shimmered in utopian light. Those days only happen when the temperature drops below the triple-digits, so that rules out the summer months. Since it was discernibly cooler, hot air balloons dotted the sky. Rocky mountain foothills struck a dramatic pose against the Technicolor blue. Ancient saguaros raised their arms in praise of creation. The sun was a friend and not the oppressor it would become a few months later. Temperatures hovered in the 70s, meaning no need for climate control. In other words: desert perfection. Arizona in springtime.

I walked in the door at the end of my workday (which, on a day like that, was probably about 2 p.m. Life is short, and the desert spring, even shorter). I was met at the door by a bouncing 3-year-old. She was holding a yellow teddy bear that I'd never seen before. "Mommy! The man dropped this to me from the sky!"

"Um . . . OK," I responded lamely, wondering what fun game I had missed. My husband appeared behind her. "No really, a guy dropped it to her from the sky," he said.

From a motorized parasail, to be exact. This is what people do for fun in desert utopia. They retire, they buy things that fly, and then they find some nice piece of wilderness preserve, and arm themselves with toys in case they see kids hanging around in the backyards that border the area. We lived at the edge of one such wilderness area—an expansive, hundred-acre desert preserve. Mountains, trails, coyotes, hot air balloons landing in our backyard—the whole bit.

So, as the story goes, the kids were playing in the backyard. They were probably mostly naked, because when you're a toddler and you live in the desert, life is a clothing-optional experience. (Some other time I'll tell you about when my son, at 2 years old, fell on top of a cactus. Completely naked. Then tried to grab it to pull himself up. Then got mad and hit the thing. But that probably does not go in a chapter about joy.)

Anyway, my naked offspring heard the low hum of a motorized flying machine and ran out to wave at it. Because that's what you do when you're a naked desert baby. The thing swooped low, the driver waving back at them, then circled back around, then near the house, even lower this time, and from there, the driver reached out and dropped, into the hands of an ecstatic girl child, the stuffed yellow bear that would go on to become family legend.

Even if, a couple hours later, I was rescuing that yellow bear from the dog, who seemed to think it was his, I put it safely out of reach in a cabinet. It wasn't the two-dollar toy that I wanted to preserve, but the story itself. Which is a good thing because, between the dog and the two toddlers, that cheapo made-in-China bear did not survive.

The good news is, they do remember—however vaguely. And for that I am grateful. Because how often does an unexpected joy like that come falling, literally, from the sky, and into your very hands?

Actually, it happens like that all the time. In fact, that may be the only way that joy comes to us. Spontaneously and without planning or manipulation on our part. Which is ironic, because we wind up spending much of our time and resources trying to arrange for joy to visit us. But joy cannot always be managed. It is a living thing without agenda.

In other seasons, that desert starts to look a little less like paradise, and a little more like something out of Dante. Hot and dry, unmerciful sun, visible waves of misery rising out of the dust. Everywhere, dust. The air does not move. But then, after months of thirsty waiting, it starts to *rain*. Not a smattering tease, but a long, soaking mercy that we'd scarcely dared to dream about in the weeks before. As welcome as a yellow bear in springtime—and as much a surprise to our parched senses—it speaks of joy beyond all dreaming, and breathes life back into the wasted earth.

We run out to meet it, and the blessing falls into our very hands. And I'm reminded that gifts from the sky are more precious when they are rare—though maybe they are not so rare as I'd once imagined.

PRACTICING JOY AT HOME

As a parent, it is a spiritual discipline to be fully present for those in-between moments of joy. And it really does take discipline, sometimes, to let the urgency of a task take a backseat to, say, the dance party happening in the living room, the bubbles being blown on the back porch, or the epic fort being built upstairs. What's that? They're using every pillow and blanket in the house and it will take hours of prodding to make them clean it up and even then it will require me to do the last half myself because I am so tired of making people do things? Yes, and this is why joy takes discipline.

So yes, as a parent, it is my job sometimes to just bear witness to the joy. Let it unfold around me—without trying to plan or contrive it, messy though it may be—and mark its presence with my own.

As a pastor, my job is much the same: all the sermon prepping, meeting sitting, and vision casting is really just creating a space for some organic thing to take shape. The joy of life in community is a living, breathing body of its own. It often visits us in spite of our best efforts to leave it off of the agenda. And sometimes, when the space for it has been lovingly cultivated—or blessedly left empty—it unfolds out of the ashes.

One of the greatest gifts of ministry is the invitation to walk alongside people when they are in the valley. And greater still is being able to witness the ways in which people still find joy, even in those places of darkness and suffering.

I could cite so many examples of the ways people walk gracefully through this tension, and yet I don't feel they are my stories to tell. But it is a privilege beyond words to witness the ways people of faith care for each other in times of shared loss; the ways in which families continue to live fully and lovingly together, even when they are reeling from a great schism in their universe; and the ways individuals act in loving and giving ways, even when they are, themselves, living through a great deal of suffering. That place of joy touching devastation has perhaps the most transformative potential of all human experience.

Though we can't control or manipulate joy itself, the space it occupies can be cultivated. Through prayer and study of Scripture, through the life of community, and in a thousand little choices we make every day we embrace joy in spite of circumstances to the contrary. We carve out that space when we dance, sing, write, and create together.

When my brother Chris was 15, he broke his leg—playing *tennis* of all things. (I felt strongly that he needed a better story for such a dramatic injury, but alas, there were witnesses, so what can you do?) This happened toward the end of the school year, which meant that following reparative surgery, he faced three months of summer in a completely non-weight-bearing cast. No summer sports or job. No church camp. No youth group mission trip. No swimming. That's an awfully long summer, all things considered.

I was in my 20s and no longer living at home, so I was in and out that summer. But I remember a couple of things. The first being that, in his convalescent state, he hollered that he was unable to clean up after me as usual, so I was going to have to "pick up my own damn shoes for a while." Yes, I'm eight years older and he still cleans up after me. Ask him sometime; he'll be happy to tell you all about it.

I also remember that, every time I went by the house that summer, he was in the same place—sitting on the piano bench. Rather than lamenting his invalid state, he had decided this summer was as good a time as any to pick up lessons again.

So he played. And he played. And he played some more. For hours every day. The hymnal, the Beatles, and probably some stuff in between. He practiced all summer, and a year later, he was accepted to the Governor's School for the Arts program, a competitive statewide summer intensive. Two years after that, he was accepted into Belmont University in Nashville, Tennessee, one of the top music programs in the country. He is now a career musician with a master's degree in classical performance. He has traveled the world with the Broadway musical *Rain: A Tribute to the Beatles*. He has toured the country with Alton Brown, as his composer/accompanist. He has started his own music company, he has composed and recorded an album, and he plays church gigs all over Nashville. You know, in his free time.

I'm not just bragging. OK, maybe bragging just the tiniest bit. But mostly I'm pointing to how a place of literal brokenness turned out to be creative space. Following that injury, the sudden emptiness of the season before him seemed not like a threat or a gaping void, but an invitation to some new kind of life. No way could he have known, when he picked up a level-one "Learn to Play" book, that he was picking up a critical piece of the rest of his life. But choosing a creative path in response to any kind of crisis or setback is always an invitation to new life, as yet unseen.

And joy comes in the morning, just on the other side of all that emptiness.

Such a creative and life-giving approach is not always our first response to a crisis. I know that the space for my brother to walk into that new life, even with a broken leg, was cultivated by years and years of seeing our mother sit at the organ every Sunday. Of hearing her practice those hymns at home on the piano throughout the week. It was in the music that was always playing in the background of our lives, whether it was coming from the basement stereo, the car radio, or the high school choir—a formative experience for Chris and me both, in our respective eras. Ultimately, we are shaped by our surroundings in so many ways. The ability to cope with loss, to answer struggle with creativity, and to find joy in all kinds of circumstances is a transformative gift that we internalize all along the way.

The good news is that we don't have to be extraordinary artists, musicians, or master Lego builders to make space for joy. We are created in the image of God, and therefore, creative partners with God. We were made with joy, and *for* joy. Caring for the earth, caring for children and neighbors, or just being still in nature or participating in worship—these are the small ways we step into that creative calling. Whether building with blocks, baking bread, caring for a garden, practicing music, or playing Minecraft, whatever we engage with a spirit of joy opens space for connection to God and other.

PRACTICING JOY IN COMMUNITY

One small town in Kentucky found how placing value on creativity, and emphasizing the practice of creative community,
brought life to a place of emptiness and decline.

The once-impressive neighborhood was called Lowertown—
it was just downriver of downtown Paducah, Kentucky. If you
don't know your Kentucky geography, let me just tell you—
Paducah is not "small town" compared to where I come from.
But it is definitely not Louisville, either. And geographically
speaking, it is basically Missouri.

"Lowertown," named for its proximity to the rest of town,
was beautiful and elegant. Until it wasn't. You know how it
goes: drugs, graffiti, and falling-apart buildings, with lots of
dark corners to cloak the violence.

In an effort to rebuild that part of town, the city decided to
make Lowertown an Arts District. And instead of just fixing
up some retail space, putting it up for lease, and hoping for
some quality artists, they went another route. In the year 2000,
they developed an Artist Relocation Program—yes, in a small
town in western Kentucky, that is actually a thing—and they
extended an invitation to artists from all over the country, saying you can buy a plot of land or an old house for *one dollar*. If
you can fix it—you can have it. If you can make some attempt
to make this place beautiful again—it's yours.

Over the next few years, those artists came. They came
from Maryland and California and everywhere in between.
They bought those corners, those old houses, those abandoned
apartments. They moved in and commenced creating. They
turned the lights back on. Now that corner of town is filled
with people who create, display, and sell beautiful works of art.
Other people are pouring money into that end of town now,
because they want to be in proximity to all the coolness. And
it is a thriving burg with spirit and working streetlights. Not to
mention—art. Lots and lots of art.[1]

I love this story of how one community rallied, in creative
spirit, and empowered a wave of renewal that reached far

beyond their own neighborhood. I refer to it often in sermons because it embodies so well the kind of transformative effect that we can each have on our surroundings, if we cultivate the space for creative living, being, and problem-solving together. Together we explore the ways we can weather the shifting needs and expectations of our members and neighbors in ways that joyfully partner with God in a creative spirit of community.

I was spending a summer morning with the women from my husband's side of the family—mother-in-law, sisters-in-law, aunts, cousins, and my own kids. We were crammed into two vans for the trek across Western Kentucky backroads, visiting the Amish farmer's markets in the area.

I've always thought that the Amish really have some stuff figured out. They know how to live simply. They are all about the peace *and* the nonviolence—in practice and in theory. They make *the best bread.* And jam, and casseroles, and not to mention they grow some killer tomatoes, which, when I was living in the desert, were entirely worth the long trip home. My kingdom for a tomato sandwich . . .

And so it was a beautiful morning, and I was enjoying being with my people and dwelling in the peace of God's country and good produce and the loving community that so obviously has it together in a way that we less-evolved consumers do not.

And then, I casually picked up the tract lying by the check-out counter.

Picture the worst, most graphic, and horrifying fire-and-brimstone propaganda that you've ever encountered, and crank up the Stephen King factor times about a hundred. That's what this was. "DO YOU KNOW WHERE YOU'RE GOING WHEN YOU DIE??" Followed by comic book depictions of unfortunate creatures burning for eternity in a lake of hellfire.

I did a double take. I read the stuff again. Like the proverbial train wreck effect, I was unable to look away from the carnage. Then I took in the scene around me—beautiful farm country, friends and family working together, big, lush, actually red tomatoes. It just didn't add up. All around me was the joy of creation, but here on this small piece of paper was an expression of their most deeply held beliefs. Dark and foreboding. And utterly without joy.

Let me be quick to say, I do not want to pin the entirety of Amish beliefs and traditions on this one unfortunate tract that I picked up at a roadside stand in Kentucky. Just like I wouldn't want anyone to judge all mainline Christians by what they might encounter at a rural church in my hometown, on the other end of the state.

But that moment stands out in my mind because it powerfully captures the disconnect between speaking one set of values and embodying another. How can one speak of a joyful, loving faith out of one side of the mouth—and preach about this terrifying, vindictive God out of the other?

I wondered about those girls, as they bagged up our beautiful ears of corn. I wondered if, within that narrative of judgment, fear, and ultimate violence, there was room for joy in their faith.

I remembered hearing about a court case in Arizona several years before. A mother was brought up on charges of emotional abuse, because her daughter frequently tried to evangelize the other children at school. That sounds absurd, and you'd better believe it was a big controversy in the local faith community. But it wasn't that simple. This poor girl was not just trying to tell people about Jesus; she would frequently narrate, in gross detail, the eternal suffering and damnation that awaited these souls, if they didn't get on the right path now. She so firmly believed in the hell she espoused, she would become distraught if she felt her message wasn't getting through.

This was a child. One who carried the burden of a fearful narrative, internalized at a very young age. I often wonder what happened to that child and her family, but I also know they are one of many who dwell in that culture of shadow cast by fear.

As people of faith in this new millennium, it is crucial—for the survival of Christianity, and for the transformation of God's becoming kingdom—that we learn to extract our narrative from that one and offer up a more joyful and life-giving path to live

in this way of Jesus. Organized religion often tends to emphasize the way of absolutes, the way of being right, and ultimately,
the way of control. It is largely a matter of self-interest, because
this way of black-and-white, in-or-out thinking has long served
to preserve the institution. But as with any kind of relationship,
one so controlling can quickly become abusive.

To cling to such a totalitarian faith is not only abusive to
the people who practice it; it is an abuse of the Christian story
itself. A story that is rooted in the joy of resurrection, and all
the life-giving potential of God's creative genius.

So how do we, contemporary people of faith, reclaim a way
of living that narrative that points to the joy inherent in our
very being, and empowers our people with God's transforming
gifts of creative mercy?

Sometimes, that has as much to do with what we don't
teach, as what we do.

To that end, our children's ministry team at church has a
motto: "Don't teach them anything they'll have to unlearn later."

As co-creators with God, one of our greatest callings is the
nurture of young people in the faith. A big part of that is telling the story of a faith that celebrates life, seeking relationships
that honor God and other. The idea that there is eternal damnation lurking in the future if we don't walk the line—and
pray exactly the right prayer, using the institutionally approved
words, while overseen by the proper church authorities, while
holding our noses just right—that story is one that we know
well. But there is no room for it in the work of loving children
into the fullness of life.

As a pastor, I've walked alongside countless adults who
are trying to unlearn that toxic narrative from rigid childhood teachings. At best, it leads people to abandon faith, and
the faith community altogether. At worst, it leads to anxiety,
depression, anger, and a general bitterness toward the world.
Whatever you believe about life and death, sin and salvation,
the long-term spiritual effects of a spiritual upbringing cen-
tered on hell and damnation cannot be examined and called
good. Furthermore, it cannot be denied that a faith forged

in fearfulness will never have the depth and purpose of faith rooted in love, grace, and deep joy.

Perhaps the most life-giving element we can add to faith—at any age—is some open space. Provide some room for doubt without fear of retribution; a certain comfort level with the unknown and the ability to embrace all the mystery of God, so that change and uncertainty and even death are not such frightening prospects. A healthy community learns to live with and engage difficult questions—rather than committing all of the precise answers to illustrated tract form. Without the relentless pressure to live within rigid parameters of belief, there is room to creatively engage questions in a way that embraces the joy of the divine.

You can't exactly measure how well a faith community is living into questions and making space for creative engagement and mystery, but I know the fruits when I see them.

One day my kids were playing church. Because that's what PKs (preachers' kids) do at home, when they aren't *building liquor stores with their toys*. After they'd been at it a while, they came and got me and told me that I needed to come for a meeting.

Dang it. I do not want to go to church meetings at home. On my day off. But I obliged.

My daughter was holding court with a blue binder, full of notes. I wondered if I was at a worship committee meeting? Stewardship and finance? Perhaps the planning team for Vacation Bible School?

As it happened, I had stumbled into the first discernment stages of a new church plant. In that binder were notes, drawings, an order of worship, and, of course, plans for the grand opening picnic.

The longer I sat through this meeting, the more I wanted to see this church happen in real life. Much of the discussion at that "meeting" had to do with the physical space of the new church. (I kept my mouth shut about the realities of capital campaigns, fundraising, and budget meetings. Let them keep their innocence awhile yet, I thought.) They discussed how many chairs we would need. They had ideas about everything from an outdoor treehouse and tire swing to a prayer garden and steeple bells. Then my daughter casually mentioned "and, you know, a place for the animals to have Communion."

That struck me as just about the sweetest thing I'd ever heard so I pried her for more information about the critter Communion station. "Like, what does it look like? Is it outside, or in the sanctuary? Does somebody stand there and serve them, like hold the cup and everything?" I had a million questions.

But she just looked at me like I was dense and said "Well, you know . . . like how we do on Sundays."

And then I figured out where she was getting this. After worship on Sundays, while the servers for the day are cleaning up the sanctuary, a few of the kids always take the leftover Communion bread outside and throw it into the garden to feed the birds.

This idea of serving Communion to the animals was not some childish whim she had dreamed up on her own. It's what she's been doing forever. What all of the kids at our church have been doing forever. While we thought they were disposing of leftovers—or at best, feeding the birds—they have been blessing the elements and serving our neighbors—the deer, the squirrels, the rabbits, and I guess the birds of the air as well. Not scattering throwaway crumbs, but the sanctified bread of life.

That idea from my kids' pretend church meeting was just about the most joyful, at-one-with-creation image of worship and church life I'd ever witnessed. And it just landed on wings of its own. I didn't have to do a thing.

I am grateful for a church family that nurtures children in this spirit of love and care for the earth. For a gospel life that is not fraught with anxiousness and fear and judgment; that leaves space for divine mystery and surprise; and that invites frequent encounters with the Joyful Divine, in all its creative glory.

JOY IN SCRIPTURE

Between the edge of the Red Sea and the edge of desert wilderness, there was a chasm of uncertainty. Yes, God had delivered the Israelites safely from the Egyptian army in pursuit, but now what? What would they eat? Where would they sleep? Where would they worship? They didn't know yet about tents in the desert, and manna, and "a pillar of cloud to lead them." And yet . . . Miriam danced.

She invited a spirit of celebration into what could have been a terrifying time. She created a way for her family and community to find joy in all the open space before them; thinking not of what they had lost, but only of the promise that God had put before them.

This is one of many stories in Scripture that show what it means to live into the blank space in joyful anticipation of what God might do next. In these moments, we begin to see that space not as emptiness, but as a blank canvas for the Holy Spirit to do a new thing. This doesn't diminish real loss or hardship, but it does prepare us to glimpse new life that is unfolding in the meantime.

If we still doubt that a creative spirit holds the power to transform darkness into light, we have only to flip through all the references to music, dance, and beauty that the Psalms hold. Or the images of art and artistry that appear consistently throughout the biblical story. God is a potter, and we the clay on the wheel; God is a gardener, and we are apprentices, all the earth waiting to be tended by us. In each of these divine expressions, it is clear that God takes joy in shaping, crafting, and birthing the world. And calls us to go and do likewise.

AROUND THE TABLE:
QUESTIONS FOR DISCUSSION

1. What does your family like to create together?
2. How do you practice joy as a family and in community?
3. Can you think of a time when your church (or community) faced uncertainty with creative problem solving?
4. Describe some glimpses of joy that you have seen in a simple moment, or in the midst of an otherwise difficult time.

6

Justice: More than Mercy

We say it's important. We cite Scripture that tells us it's important. But we do not always know how to talk about it. Especially when our justice system itself is so entrenched in a toxic quagmire of racism and violence. Especially if we've never been on the receiving end of this systemic dysfunction.

Last summer, twelve Dallas police officers were shot during what was supposed to be a peaceful protest. The protest was one of many to emerge, nationwide, in the wake of two successive police killings of black men: Alton Sterling in Louisiana, and Philando Castile in Minnesota. Those two horrific acts of violence were earthquakes—small, local tremors that swept across the countryside over the course of a day, landing in Dallas as a tsunami of violence and rage.

Sadly, police officers shooting black men in what appeared to be an excess of force were not extraordinary incidents. It just so happened that these two shootings occurred in quick succession, were both caught on video, and were both highly publicized. With many details still unknown and still under investigation, the public perception is one of unjustified police brutality. And it is nothing new.

I know police officers who go to work every day, wearing their authority with compassion and care, placing their lives on the line for the safety of the public. Most cops are good cops.

Perhaps that is why the few who abuse that authority so rarely face consequences. Perhaps that is why, in the wake of incidents like these, the public is so quick to say "there must have been a reason." Perhaps that is why the media is so quick to dig up a years-old mug shot of the victim. And why fellow officers rush to the defense, saying, "You don't know what it's like out there, to have your life on the line every day."

They're right, I don't. And unless you are a police officer, you probably don't either. But, I'm coming to realize, black people do know what it's like to have their lives on the line. People of color know, and have always known, that they are in danger every day of being mistaken for a dangerous criminal; that a busted tail light, or the wearing of a hoodie, or a legally concealed weapon, or an openly carried toy gun, can get them shot dead in the street, in front of their children.

The days following those incidents—and the continued violence by police and against police—marked just a few of the many days that find me struggling to talk about justice. What it means, what it looks like, who's in charge of enacting it. Because I don't know what it's like to be a black person in this country. I do not know what the solution is, but I know that it's going to take white people learning to overcome the visceral, defensive reaction we often display when the topic of racism comes up. It also means that officers who take innocent lives, when their own are in no clear danger, must be prosecuted. It is going to take a great deal of effort to root out the language of "they must have had a reason," and "that guy probably did something bad at some point and had it coming" (the message clearly implied when the media dredge up old mug shots).

But more than just prosecuting the events themselves, we are called to address the hateful narrative that this nation has harbored against people of color for centuries. Far from being

a trickle from the ancient past, it is a rushing river—the flood-
gates of which have been opened by the tone of recent political
rhetoric.

So what do we do now? Other than to employ a hashtag and
"demand justice" on social media, and try not to vote for leaders who intentionally stoke the fires of racial tension for their
own political gain? I do not know. It's something I struggle
with daily.

I find great hope, however, in knowing how many others struggle too. Because there is transformative power in the
struggle.

My friend Rev. Chris Furr, pastor of Covenant Christian
Church in Cary, North Carolina, had this to say:

> I watched two videos yesterday that I would have preferred
> not to see. Alton Sterling's son crying for his daddy in front
> of a crowd of reporters, and the second eyewitness video of
> the shooting. If you are like me, you do not want to watch.
> This is precisely why you must.
>
> It is easy to pass by hurt you think is not yours to feel. A
> lawyer once asked Jesus how he could know who his neigh-
> bor is, and in response Jesus told a story about a man left for
> dead along the road, while others passed by. Perhaps some
> kept going because they would not see that treating some as
> less than human makes us all less than human. Perhaps they
> seized the privilege of not seeing, which is the privilege of
> those not left by the road themselves. This is its own kind
> of death, a spiritual one.
>
> In the end, Jesus turned the question around. "Which
> do you think was a neighbor to the man?" The question
> isn't about who your neighbor is. That question assumes
> there is pain or injustice that can be ignored, if the victim is
> not in your proximity.
>
> The question is, what kind of neighbor are you—to
> those who have been left for dead?
>
> How much longer will we pass by?

The privilege of not seeing . . . What a searingly true kind of
blindness that is. And for many of us, it is a blindness with

multiple layers. We can afford to "not see" the injustices of race if our skin color has never been a liability; you might choose to "not see" gender inequality if you are a man. We ignore economic injustice every day, remaining compliant in the unjust system. We can recuse ourselves from the struggle for marriage equality, if our marriage is already recognized by the law. The list goes on, but the bottom line remains: when it comes to matters of justice, the privilege of not seeing is perhaps *the* original sin. The small localized tremor, the chaos all around us, and the resulting, global tsunami.

How do we talk to our children about injustice, when we so scarcely understand it ourselves? When we know our way of life to be complicit in perpetuating it? As is so often the case, I do not have the answer. At least, not a single, definitive answer. What I do know is that these conversations with our kids begin with a fundamental "seeing": choosing to recognize the ways in which our playing pieces don't always start from the same space on the board game. These conversations need to start early and with intention. Often, we can wait for the teaching moment to present itself; or, better yet, trust that our children have their own kind of "seeing" that is often superior to our own, and know that they will invite us into the conversation when they are ready to have it.

My daughter and her cousin Taylee are only a few months apart in age. They are the oldest grandchildren in a very large family; for many years they were the only girls among a pack of grandsons, and they have basically been best friends since birth. Together, these girls choreograph synchronized dance routines, wear matching outfits whenever possible, and get identical toys at Christmas. They sleep in the same bed, they share straws, they speak in code.

And it has never once occurred to them that there is any difference between them—even though Taylee is biracial. It has never occurred to them that, to some people's eyes, they do not look like family. I've always been grateful that skin color is not even on the radar for them.

So maybe at some level, I always thought the depth of that relationship could take the place of difficult conversations about race. That her closeness to a person with darker skin would teach her all she needs to know about justice and equality. But now I know otherwise. Now I know that deep love for her cousin, and a certain privileged blindness to her skin color, is not enough.

A couple of years ago, Harper came home from kindergarten one day telling me all about Martin Luther King Jr. She sang a little song, and told me the story; we talked about water fountains and buses, and what is fair and what is not. I was impressed that they were starting this in public school so early (in Kansas even, where we are lately not so much known for our progressive ways). With her interest thus piqued, I marched her right to the library and got some books about MLK and the civil rights movement. And the next year, for Black History Month, we did the same thing.

Around the same time, the kids overheard my husband and I talking about a certain nasty presidential race, and a certain candidate whose use of incendiary speech bore not-so-subtle racist undertones. They occasionally pick up on our outrage. *Why don't we want him to be president?* Oh, kidletts . . . where to begin? I tried to explain, in age-appropriate ways, that some people who like this candidate want things to be more like they used to be . . . *sort of like back in MLK's time,* was the best way I could think of to describe it. That was not entirely accurate, and was utterly lacking in nuance, but it was the best way I could think to help them understand, in the context of a history they sort of know about.

"Sort of" turned out to be a critical distinction.

About a week after that conversation, I picked my daughter up from school, and she came out chatting with friends as usual. On the walk home, she tells me that she was talking to one of her friends (who is African American) about the presidential race. *Uh-oh.*

"So I told her," she said, "if that one guy is president and everything is like MLK times again, I told her not to worry—I will take good care of her."

Insert horrified mom face here.

The sentiment may be admirable, at a basic 7-year-old level. But on the whole, I was disturbed. Because, beneath the first grade understanding of civil rights, there lies an uncomfortable assumption that, if this whole democracy thing falls apart, our family—middle-class white people—will be the ones holding the cards. We will be the ones empowered to "take care of" (or not) the people whose rights have been removed. We will be called to kindness and compassion, by virtue of our authoritative place in history. But not to worry—because we will not abuse that power like people in the past have done.

"We will take good care of you."

And that's privilege in a nutshell. The misconception that we can somehow be free when others are not. That we can learn to accept some inevitable inequality, as long as we are kind about it.

In that moment, which thread do you start pulling at first?

First off, some further conversation revealed that she has confused elements of the civil rights movement with elements of the Civil War. So there were some gaps in history to sort out.

"And also," I said, working to extract the larger point from the confusing political stuff, "if you want to take care of people—and I'm glad that you do—then what we really want is for everyone to have all the same chances, all the same rights. That's the only way it can ever be fair. That way is better for everybody."

It's not her fault. Her heart—her huge, 7-year-old, vegetarian heart—is clearly in the right place. *Hey, if the world goes all to hell and the bad people get in charge, I'll take care of my people!* I get it. But it also alerted me to a major mom fail. While I have talked to my kids about racism, in the most basic ways, I have failed to address privilege—and the thousand little ways that the world is made easier for them than it is for their cousin, and some of their friends.

Isn't that the story of life in this country? We thought we had stamped out racism because the law has made things "fair," and we all are best friends some days, and everything is "nice" and "fine."

But recently, with the white outrage stemming from having a black president in office; the currents of violence that continue to ripple in small and large ways every day; and the sludge of bigotry dredged up from the bottom of the pool in an election year; it's clear that this is the world we live in, and we can't ignore this part of our narrative anymore. Not everything is as "nice" and "fine" as we like to think.

If there is an upside to the increasing vitriol of our political scene, I guess it would be the invitation it provides faithful people to enter into deep and difficult conversations about our communal life together. And for the urgency that many of us suddenly feel to do better with our own children; to not be one more generation of "post-racial Americans," but instead learn to hear and be present to the struggles of our neighbors.

As I talked to my daughter that day, I had an epiphany of time and space. Yes, she had distorted a couple of major moments in history, but the biggest gap in her education was not a missing piece of the past—it was missing pieces of present reality that really confused her. When we talk about rights and freedom, she is thinking just about the law of the land; but what we are really talking about is the subconscious of an entire culture.

The first time I heard the term "environmental racism," I thought it meant a scenario wherein one becomes a racist by product of living in a racist community. Having grown up in southeastern Kentucky, I know that to be a true phenomenon—though perhaps not one named by anthropologists. However, that's not what it means. Environmental racism is the reality that lower income neighborhoods—particularly, neighborhoods largely populated by people of color—are far more susceptible to living with poor air quality, undrinkable water, the eyesores of urban decay, and other living conditions that those with more resources would find unacceptable.

In 2014, the Christian Church, Disciples of Christ, made a statement about environmental racism; it was a resolution to study the issue, to speak out against it, and to engage in the movement for change. So I was just beginning to learn about what it meant and what we should do about it, and just starting to talk about it at my church, when life offered us a living, real-time example of what it looks like: Flint, Michigan.

It must be something in the water. That's usually what people say when a common trend takes hold of a community. Like when a bunch of women in the same church get pregnant at the same time, or an extended family has a big wave of weddings in one summer, or a bunch of houses in the neighborhood go on the market at the same time.

But in Flint—a population that, according to recent census info, is nearly 60 percent African American—that something in the water was lead. That is no folksy appellation. It is a real-life iteration of white privilege, and a painful expression of how real and present racism is in our culture. It is cloudy; it is dirty; it is poison. And in the case of Flint, somebody, somewhere knew about it and did nothing. Officials at both state and local levels were notified numerous times, by numerous bodies, that there was something wrong with the new water supply—which the town switched to in spring of 2014 as a cost-saving measure—leading to a lead-poisoning epidemic among children in the community.

Prior to the public scandal, state officials heard concerns of many citizens about the bad taste and muddy color of the water. In nearly every case, they deferred to local authorities. Local authorities heard concerns. And from there, that's where the waters get murky, so to speak. All the ambiguity about whose job it was to ensure clean water for the community makes it a lot harder to prosecute someone. The criminal negligence becomes the product of a "broken system"; an invisible criminal with no name, face, or voting record.

While this sort of thing can happen anywhere, it is far more likely to happen in impoverished areas, and in places with higher minority populations. This would not happen in a predominantly white and wealthy suburb in America. It just wouldn't. Or at least, it wouldn't get this far and have such far-reaching impact before there was a public outcry.

In the days following the immediate crisis, many local organizations, including churches from my own denomination, joined forces to get clean water to the people of Flint. This was good and important work, to be sure. The immediate need was for clean, safe water so that people could get on with life in the midst of this crisis. But getting water to thirsty people is not justice.

Getting water to people who need water, in the short term, is the work of mercy. As we discussed in previous chapters, this is an important value to practice as well. But it is not the same thing as justice. *Mercy is giving water to thirsty people; justice is ensuring that all people have access to clean water.*

The work of mercy and justice often live and work alongside each other. But the act of service does not transform the deeper reality; the work of justice does.

As parents and community charged with raising the next generation of Jesus' disciples, we live in this tension, and seek to balance these two related but (different) callings: to show compassion, and to live justly.

Deliver the water—but fix the source.

PRACTICING JUSTICE IN COMMUNITY

It will be hard. It will be awkward. You'd better believe we are going to screw this up. But we can't just trust that our kids' relationships with people who are different from them will teach them everything they need to know about creating a more just world.

We can't just assume that by the time they are grown up the world will have moved past all this. And we can't just trust that a few meaningful friendships with people of other races will change the game in meaningful ways. The transformative work of relationship takes place in community—and I am glad to have a village for those difficult conversations.

In the meantime, there are ways that we can also embody and enact the kinds of justice we desire for the world, in our own small circles of connection.

Of course, once we begin pulling at the threads of racial and economic injustice, we acknowledge that those threads are connected to so many other social ills. A truly just worldview examines economic injustice, gender equality, prejudice against the LGBT community, immigrants, Muslims . . . the list goes on and on. There are so many broken places where parts of our humanity can fall between the cracks. So many places where the privilege of "not seeing" makes us complicit in sins of inequality.

Perhaps the most important lesson for children, then, is to acknowledge the hand they are holding—to name and recognize the ways in which their lives might be inherently easier because of something they have very little control over. If they're holding more cards than a friend, a neighbor, or a cousin, then they need to have that named for them and understand their role in shifting the narrative. Not just sharing what they have, but questioning why the system itself is so inherently broken.

The role of the faith community, then, is to help with that work of articulation, and also to draw us into relationship with those who are not distinctly "like us." That can be difficult to do when our churches are so often direct reflections of our neighborhoods—so in terms of economy, race, and even life stage we often find ourselves sitting in worship with those who look a lot like us. If we desire justice that is more than spoken, we may have to reach beyond our immediate neighbors to build transformative relationships.

In deep listening, hard questions, uncomfortable territory—those thin places where we don't know the answers—those are holy places where we know God has moved close and might show us something new. Where our own words end, God's mercy can move into the void.

For the congregation that I serve, interfaith dialogue is a big part of that work. We partner with a Turkish cultural center in our neighborhood. Some of our members meet in homes for dinner and conversation; we join them in their work of welcoming refugees to our city, specifically those coming from the Middle East. One of their leaders brought her daughters to speak to our children's Sunday school one week, when we were doing a series with them about world religions.

Each year, we host a Ramadan fast-breaking feast for members of our community and theirs. Well, I say "host." The truth is, we just unlock the doors and maybe put the coffee on. Then they show up with the most delicious food—loads of it, of course. And we all enjoy a wonderful meal together.

At these gatherings, I'm always struck by this one thing. Our Muslim friends have been fasting all day, having breakfast before sunrise and then waiting until after sunset for dinner. (And in the summer months, sunset is about 9 p.m.) Our folks, on the other hand, do well if we skipped snacks between lunch and this late-night feast. And yet—our guests insist that we go first.

We are the hosts—it's our house, shouldn't our guests go first?

We are the hosts—shouldn't we bring the food?

We are the hosts—shouldn't we do something more than just show up and enjoy all this goodness?

There's some kind of parable there, I'm certain of it.

Or maybe it's just a living example of the power of real relationship, versus the ease of abstraction that the world so often invites us to. It's an illustration of the abundance, transformative grace, and overwhelming generosity that God has offered us—a fullness of life that is meant to be shared. This is justice.

We try to take that same relational approach to all of our mission work, not just sharing our resources, but believing it is only in relationship that we will transform the world. I do not mean, in any way, to pretend that we've got this figured out. But I do find this a healthier approach to doing mission—and a more fruitful way of life for the church—than traditional models of service.

There is a small mountain village in El Salvador, near the border of Honduras, called El Higueral. They were recovering from the civil war in that region at the same time our youngish church was in formation, and so our communities formed a sister village relationship. We have tried to walk alongside them ever since, learning from each other—but much like our connection with the Muslim community, it feels a lot like us relying on their hospitality when we go to visit, and feeling like what we offer in return is kind of thin. They house us, feed us, and roast fresh coffee for our morning visit. The coffee is worth the price of admission (or at least the price of air travel) every single time. The life we experience there is so full of grace and goodness—and yet, it is we who have been given so much. We who have freedom to come and go across borders as we please, we who have access to education and healthcare (much as we complain about its worthiness), and we who have always known the relative safety of democracy.

In return, we support sustainable development in their village; we've helped install an irrigation system, a community oven, a computer lab with Internet; we helped build a church (which is Catholic, because they are) and we help pay tuition and travel for youth who want to attend high school in the neighboring town.

This seems to be a pattern.

We are the ones with privilege—shouldn't they be our guests and go first?

They are the hosts—it is their joy to feed us.

We are as privileged guests—shouldn't we do something more than just show up and enjoy all this goodness?

We are still learning to do the work of accompaniment: "mission" work that honors relationship and functions in real understanding. We try to work in this same model with local agencies we serve as well. But in all this, there is one central truth that embodies our practice of justice: *Bring water, but fix the source.*

JUSTICE IN SCRIPTURE

The term Good Samaritan has become so cliché in our culture that we frequently hear it tossed around on the evening news. "Good Samaritan Saves Man from Burning Vehicle!" "Good

Samaritan Buys Christmas Gifts for Needy Family!" "Good
Samaritan Gets Cat Out of Tree!"

That last one must be a really slow news day. Still, it's a
term we hear all the time, in the most casual reference to someone doing a good thing. But lifting that image out of context
diminishes much of its meaning—which is so often the case
with Scripture. A Samaritan in Jesus' time was an outcast, one
who was deeply mistrusted by the public at large. The fact that
such a character wound up being the good guy in this story—
over and above the people who should have been the good
guys—adds a great deal of depth to the lesson. Casually referring to any do-gooder as a "good Samaritan" is an excellent
lesson in missing the point.

So, who is my neighbor? Maybe it's not who you think.

And that's what Jesus taught, with every miracle, every healing, every parable. Neighbor is not about proximity. Neighbor
is about who's been left out. Who's been sent out to the wilderness, excluded from the table, left by the side of the road for
dead? That's your neighbor. That's who you are called to reach
with the good news, and not in a "Do you have a relationship
with Jesus Christ?" kind of way. But in a transformative and
relational kind of way.

The work of justice, then, calls for a radical, intentional
neighboring of all creation. Connecting in a way that deep-
ens our understanding of human struggle and division, and
restores people to each other. Not just restored life; but restored
connection.

Ever notice that when Jesus heals someone, he doesn't just
fix what's hurting them physically? He also restores them to
community and relationship. Think about it.

Bring water. But also fix the source.

That's because God's kind of justice is restorative, not
retributive. In fact, human notions of retributive justice are
the antithesis of God's dream for creation. But God's kind of
justice—and the kind offered by the Third Way of Jesus—is a
broader view, not just of punishment, but of living justly.

The same is true of parables. Parables aren't just life lessons, neatly tied up with a moralistic bow. Parables are stories of the radical restoration of relationship. It's not just the story of a do-gooder helping an injured man by the side of the road. It's about *the person you least expect* being the one who best models the Jesus way. This is what my friend Chris meant when he talked about the Good Samaritan and the "privilege of not seeing." There are so many ways that we can easily walk by on the other side of the road, reading both Scripture and our own social context at a surface level. But the work of justice calls us to a deeper reading of both; an abiding knowledge of the systems in which we live; an intentional understanding of who is harmed by them; and a deep sense of calling to bring the water, but fix the source.

AROUND THE TABLE:
QUESTIONS FOR DISCUSSION

1. Read Micah 6:1–8. What are some of the ways that your family and community "Do justice, love kindness, and walk humbly with God"?
2. How does this passage demonstrate the tension, or complementary relationship, between the work of compassion and the way of just living?
3. In your immediate community, who are the most vulnerable populations? What are the immediate needs of these neighbors, and also, what would a deeper, more restorative kind of justice look like?
4. What are some barriers that your family or faith community might face in talking about privilege or systemic injustice?

7
Community: The Art of Neighboring

Whose idea was it that when you move your life across the world for a new job, at the very time when you are supposed to be knocking people's socks off at work, you are simultaneously *drowning in minutiae*? Someday, I am going to find that person who set up this order of things and send them a *strongly worded letter*. How is a person supposed to learn a new community in the midst of the chaos of finding housing, transferring insurance, securing a new hair person and mechanic, establishing care with new doctors, and getting a library card, the key to the universe? While dealing with all that soul-crushing minutiae, you also have to do the deeply spiritual work of finding the good pizza, the best burger dive, who makes the "real" Mexican food . . . and let us not forget the daunting task of touring every liquor store in town, ensuring that one's children will know how to properly design the architecture of their next Lego masterpiece.

Shortly after my family moved to Kansas City from Phoenix, a friend of mine, who had also just relocated for a new ministry call, asked me if I had any advice for getting settled into a new town. And I said something to the effect of, "Hell, I don't know, I am over here trying to remember where we packed the coffee filters and the corkscrew. And looking for socks."

In truth, it wasn't just socks we needed. It was *everything*. When you move from a warm-weather climate to a more temperate zone, you are utterly unprepared for the assault of the elements. Even if you have lived in winter-weather places before and you know, technically, what is coming, that first snow will find you layering sweatshirts, windbreakers, and other weather-inappropriate garments on your children, wondering when you are going to find time to go to the stupid mall and find them real winter clothing. You may also find that your own winter coats have disappeared over the last decade or so, the precious closet space traded out for more sundresses. So, add to the list of minutiae the securing of a whole new wardrobe for a family of four, and you might begin to near the kind of hole I found myself in, the first year in this new place of ministry.

As much as I loved my Arizona folks at the time, I was utterly unprepared for the grief of leaving them. I knew it would be hard, but I confess I was still surprised by how heavy the loss weighed on me. I'm not saying I wouldn't have left, had I known; I'm not even saying I would have done some things differently in the leaving process, because I don't know that it would have mattered. I only know that, in addition to trying to figure out a whole new life in a whole new place, I was dealing with the aftermath of what can only be described as a death. But a death with no formal liturgy to mark that passing, and no chain of folks bringing funeral casseroles to ease the pain.

Ministry can be isolating, on a good day. But in a new ministry call (which can feel much like a prolonged audition for the first year) and in a town where my family had few connections outside of the church—it was an absolute island. And not in a breezy, tropical, drinks-with-umbrellas-in-hand kind of way, either. In a raw, throat-punchy, "I-don't-quite-know-who-I-am-here" kind of way. It was a heavy time. I was not always a good parent. I was not a great wife. I was not the fun, fearless, capable leader that (I thought) I'd been in my prior call, with the right words and the established presence and the long-range vision that felt Spirit-inspired. In all honesty, and in perfect hindsight—I was a hot mess.

But here's what I found—and what you have probably found, if you've ever thrown yourself into this sort of whirlwind of rearrangement. Somewhere in the midst of all that chaos and the labyrinth of boxes and the overwhelming sea of details, you *do* find your feet in the new place. Sort of. You learn where not to drive during rush hour; you learn that the liquor stores close early on Sundays (and are totally closed on Easter—*what the heck, Kansas?*); you figure out which pizza places are going to take two hours to deliver on a weeknight; and you finally make it to the DMV. (Someday I will make it to the DMV.) The new people decide they will keep you, even if every sermon is not a work of art. The Holy Spirit learns the way to your new office. Your kids make friends with the neighbors and you finally hang some pictures on the wall and you find a new favorite coffee place.

And then . . . you live there.

While I can't exactly look back and trace how I made the move from feeling distinctly displaced to knowing that I wasn't going to blow away at the first slight breeze, I know that some of it just took time; but some of it took intention. A gradual digging into my place and deciding, with purpose, that I was going to really be here.

Those first early days here, I remember naming "grounded" as my intention in yoga. I also used that imagery in my prayer life during that season of fragility. I tried to visualize becoming a part of the landscape, and feeling as connected to the Kansas prairie as I ever did to the Kentucky mountains or the Arizona desert.

I'm still working on that. I've come to find some peace with the truth that I am just not a prairie girl at heart. I am a girl from the holler, who can also feel at home at the beach, in the desert, or way up in the Colorado Rockies—but as far as a spiritual home, the Midwest ain't it for me. Still—the work of digging in to this place served me in other ways.

Prayer and meditation were a helpful part of that journey. But really, it was the more tangible practices of "rooting" that led me to feel at peace in a new environment. It was an intentional but organic process. I went to visit local nonprofits—the ones the church is connected with, or those where individual members have connections. I got to meet the people who run them, and the people they serve. I also got involved in my kids' schools. Hear this, universe: I am not a bake sale mom, a Halloween party craft mom, or a crazy dance mom. (OK, maybe I'm a little bit that last thing.) And yet, these are all things I found myself doing/signing on/showing up for every time I turned around. Over the course of a year or two, I got to know teachers and other parents and even the crossing guard—all gradually building up the village of "who will be our people."

Mostly, I learned the spiritual discipline of talking to strangers. It's an art that preachers' kids and military spouses and other transient populations have perfected over years of idle but life-giving chit-chat; but one that I had to practice in fits and starts while learning a new congregation and, of course, trying to find my socks in the chaos. Parks, libraries, hospitals, coffee shops, the grocery store—these all became my mission field and the holy ground of my new and slowly unfolding life.

Of course, walking into a conversation with people you don't know can lead to awkward places: like that woman in the Whole Foods bar, who was clearly horrified by the whole woman minister thing. Or this other time, when I stopped for donuts on the way to church and found myself getting an earful about how the devil and, of course, the black president, are to blame for all the school shootings in our country. (And by "devil," she meant literal, actual Satan.) Mercy.

But in addition to the cans-o-worms, this spiritual work of engagement also opens doors. This is how you get from "new in town" to "I live here," and even, "We've met before." Someday, the dust will settle. And you'll look down and notice that cloud of mess beneath your feet has been hiding something: Roots.

When clergy relocate, we at least have the ready-made community of our new church family waiting for us in a new town. I cannot imagine what it's like to relocate and have to also add church shopping to that long list of things to do.

Feeling isolated and displaced, though, is not a phenomenon limited to clergy families, or even to folks who have physically relocated. We are living in a time of great cultural isolation. Just think about how many things in our daily lives are designed so that we *don't have to deal with people face-to-face:* garage door openers; fast food, coffee shops, banks, and dry cleaners all with drive-through lines; remote classrooms and work-at-home gigs; online bill pay and shopping. In fact, I recently discovered that I can order all my groceries with a few clicks and have them delivered to my door, free of charge. Even the attractiveness of the mega-church movement has much to do with the relative anonymity of a large worship gathering. You can sing the songs, pay your tithe, hear a sermon, and be back home again within 90 minutes—without having to talk to the person next to you, without ever being asked to wash the coffee cups or serve on a committee. Of course, many people involved in these kinds of communities feel deeply connected, whether through small groups or other kinds of ministry. But still; the invitation to worship undercover is there for those who want it, and it is just one more way that the rest of our lives mirror the drive-through/garage door opener phenomenon. Many of us don't know our neighbors, don't know the parents of our children's friends, and have little time for community involvement outside of on-the-clock working hours.

PRACTICING COMMUNITY AT HOME

A woman named Elizabeth had recently moved and wanted to get to know her neighbors. She was in a new house in a new area, she didn't know anyone, and her children were spending most of the summer with their father.

Some people would view that kind of space with deep sadness. Instead, Elizabeth bought a fire pit. She got some roasting sticks. And she put word out to her neighbors that, every night of the summer, she would be out there in the yard making s'mores for anyone who wanted to come over. Her goal was to "build community, one marshmallow at a time."

Everyone knows that "s'mores" is the magic word for many a life fix.

The first night she had a few neighbors come over and say hello. The next week, a few more. By the end of the summer, she had as many as *fifty people* at her house in the evenings. Not only did she get to know her new neighbors, but many of those neighbors who had lived there for years were meeting each other for the first time.[1]

Is it just me, or does that sound a lot like church? But with better communion.

The art and practice of hospitality can be both pastoral care and self-care. When you make room at your table—or your fire pit—for friends, neighbors, and strangers, there is great opportunity for transformative witness. When you invite the recently divorced or widowed neighbor, the alone-for-the-holidays church friend, or the just-moved-in-next-door family, you are ministering to the needs of those in need of a village; but you are also building your own village, and the network of people who will help sustain and support your own family. Furthermore, in those moments, children learn the art of community-building. They will need to do this time and again in their own lives—every time they join a team, when they go to college, get their first apartment, or have children of their own. There is no end to the opportunity for neighboring moments; there will be times, places, and seasons when the greatest gift that we have is the ability to open a door where others see only walls.

We belong to each other. So many things come right when we neighbors decide to be where we are, and find out who else is there with us.

NEIGHBORING AS A COMMUNITY

Practicing community in community may sound redundant— and repetitive. But as a community of faith, we practice the art of neighboring together in ways that are difficult as individuals or family units acting alone. There are many ways in which the community of faith can engage the broader community of which it is a part. These shared practices can deepen connection within the Body, while also creating space for more people at the table of fellowship.

During the season of my own relocation, I watched the unfolding refugee situation in the Middle East with a particularly raw place in my gut. We are living through one of the worst humanitarian crises of all time. And yet, the petty political posturing on our own shores continues to take precedence over the lives of millions of families—many with children—in desperate need of shelter and safety.

If my voluntary relocation—with relative mastery of the native language, an education, ready transportation, a credit card, and friends and family a day's drive away—was wreaking spiritual havoc on me, what must it be like for these weary ones, who have suffered unspeakable violence, have had loved ones wrenched from them, and got out alive, but with only the clothes on their backs? It was unthinkable.

There was so much ugliness coming from all corners of the political world, voices shouting, "We don't want them here," that my church sensed a call to get involved in refugee ministry, and work to welcome resettled families. We wanted to embody the radical hope offered by both the gospel and the U.S. Constitution. Like compassionate people all over the world, we saw those heartbreaking images of children lying dead on Turkish beaches and we said: Enough.

But where to begin?

It is complicated, legally and politically. It is complicated ideologically. It is complicated practically and logistically. And that's just on our end. With so much red tape and drama between us and people in need, it's hard to know which layer to start sifting through first. So we did what you do when you don't know what else to do: We showed up.

First, we gathered a group of interested church members. We started having regular conversations, amongst ourselves, and with local agency partners, for discernment. We learned how to best align our gifts and resources with the work already happening in our own area. We also heard the stories of people who came here as refugees, years ago, and now work with these local agencies to support others. In short—we spent time with people who have done this since before it was trendy. As with all of our mission work, we want our approach to be relational, with no toxic savior complex.

We learned, and are still learning, a great deal. For instance, we are learning what is expected of newly arrived families. For instance, that they must become largely self-sufficient within ninety days of arrival. So the most important things for them to have are affordable housing, public transportation, and language resources. None of which are readily available in the suburbs. This meant that any delusions we had of resettling a family in our neighborhood (or in our basements) went immediately out the window. As with so much of life and ministry—if we want to do this, we have to go to where the need is, not just open the door in welcome and expect the need to arrive at our threshold.

We also learned that most of these families have spent ten to twenty years in camps before coming here. Many will likely suffer from PTSD and have had little or no access to health care for years. A safe place to live is really just the beginning of what is needed to begin life again.

Perhaps the most valuable thing we learned was this: the hardest adjustment for those resettling in our country is *our cultural notion of independence.* Most refugees come from places where community is everything. Not only have they had to form these bonds for survival in a time of crisis, they also come from cultures that are very much based in family and communal living. The idea of living and working for your own autonomy is more foreign than anything else—even more so than our consumer-driven lives, our technology, our conveniences; more even than the overwhelming choices in the cereal aisle. For all of this, the gospel of "I" is most utterly confounding.

So, yes, they need clean clothes, and sheets and towels. Yes, they need food, and dishes in which to prepare that food. They need soccer balls for the kids, and diapers, and a school, and a place to learn English, and ways to get around. They need jobs and vaccinations and some lessons in how to operate basic plumbing. But more than anything, they need *people.* In a "your people will be my people, your God will be my God" kind of way.

So we learn to show up. When you come right down to it, it's all we've got.

Some of our members had the opportunity to be at the Kansas City Airport as part of an interfaith delegation to greet the first refugee family to arrive in the U.S. under the expedited "surge operation" to resettle at-risk families. They went with signs and smiles and a welcoming spirit. It wasn't much. But they showed up.

Just show up. It's all we know how to do sometimes. And maybe it's all we need to do anyway.

I got to meet one of those families that arrived late at night; stepped off the plane into a strange city; and breathed in hope that this would be a kinder land than the home they'd left. I really just carried a fruit basket.

I knocked on the door, along with another member of my church; a friend from the Muslim community, Dr. Khan, who is well practiced in these welcome visits; and a translator from a local nonprofit partner.

When we asked about a welcome gift, we were told to bring fruit and "maybe some toys for the children." No problem. We took fruit, a soccer ball, a few stuffed animals, Play-Doh, bubbles, coloring books . . . the essentials of life. We were told there were five children.

We arrived and were introduced by the translator. We were warmly gathered into the house. And *there were more than five children.* I am not sure how many, because they were running in and out the whole time and it was hard to keep track. But there were at least six. The youngest was a one-year-old baby in a puffy pink snowsuit. (It was a 60-degree day.) And there was another baby on the way.

The kids each came to see us, shy but smiling. And then they went after the clementines like it was their job. The father shook our hands. The mother hugged us. And when the grandmother came into the room, she danced. She didn't say much, but she danced over, hands waving in the air like the women I once saw worshiping in Africa. Then she embraced each of us in a bobbing kind of "I need to touch your face on both sides" way that was its own kind of dance. And its own kind of worship. She didn't say much. She didn't need to.

Every one of them, from the baby to the grandma, wore rubber flip-flops. Like the kind you buy at the Dollar Tree.

The children of refugee families start school as soon as they get vaccinated, and immediately begin learning English; they soon take on the role of primary translators for their families.

We learned that the parents in this particular family had lived in a resettlement camp in the Sudan for nearly twenty years. *Twenty years.* All of their babies were born there.

After meeting this family, I began to see our everyday, boring, so-often-taken-for-granted lives through the eyes of children born in a refugee camp. Flushing toilets. The Disney Channel. Grocery stores and Hershey bars and tiny citrus fruits and pizza bagels and baby carrots—washed, peeled, bagged, and lunchbox ready. Running water. Crayons. A shot for every kind of hepatitis. Soccer balls. A neighborhood park with a swing set.

The mercy of it all is astounding.

But also astounding is the mystery of stepping into such a dramatically different world. A world in which you are expected to become self-sufficient within thirty to ninety days, with about $1,200 to your name. That is nothing, by American standards, but that's how this works. That's what is expected of those who make it through the system. Terrorists?

They are just trying to figure out the post office. The school bus. The toaster.

"We just want to welcome you to Kansas City," said Dr. Khan. "We are all friends here. We are here for whatever you need, and we hope you will have a good and happy life here for your family."

"People who believe in God have no tribe," said Thomas, the father. "You are our family now. We are all the same."

I really just carried the oranges. I just came to the door of a stranger, with some dominoes and some bubbles. And for these folks, that's as good as family.

The mercy and the mystery . . . it's just astounding.

While the U.S. is still scrambling and fighting amongst ourselves about "maybe they're terrorists," and deciding whether or not to even let refugees settle in our cities, other countries decided to welcome first and ask questions later. Germany, especially, has been featured heavily in the global spotlight for its massive influx of refugees, and the resulting fiscal and social tensions; lingering questions about employment, housing, and healthcare make the future uncertain for these resettled populations.

But emerging from that same climate of uncertainty are some amazing stories of hope and transformation. There's one in particular that sticks with me as a powerful glimpse of kingdom potential.

The small town of Friedland is home to about 5,000 people. It used to be an active industrial area, but after reunification in 1990, things started winding down. That's a pretty common narrative of decline, in Germany and elsewhere; factories close, people leave town, or stay and die, and little by little, the streams of potential growth run dry.

What makes this particular place uncommon, though, was their path to recovery: welcoming refugees.[2]

It's a symbiotic situation: refugee families are boosting the economy, filling jobs, and compensating the population for low German birth rates. In general, a dying burg is being brought back to life. The situation is not perfect but it is a witness to the transformative power of neighboring: showing up, opening doors, and gathering around a table can have profound effects on the spirit, the community, and the world.

When in doubt—when you feel as though your village is scattered all over the country, or left behind in some previous life, or maybe just still packed in boxes—make it a point to practice sacred hospitality. When we are feeling at our lowest and most isolated, that is exactly the right time to venture out of our comfort zone and talk to strangers, have the neighbors over, or find those people who are feeling even more displaced and isolated than you might be.

Somebody, somewhere, needs nothing more than a place at your table.

NEIGHBORING IN SCRIPTURE

It's hard to know where to begin, since so much of Scripture is a model for communal living and radical neighboring. Should we start with the tribal interdependence and the formative identity shaped in the Genesis and Exodus narrative? Or skip on over to the early church in Acts, where the people "shared all things in common"?

How about we go right to the middle—the heart of everything—and visit the Communion Table?

On the eve of a great schism, Jesus gathered his beloveds. It didn't matter that the coming betrayal, arrest, and death was a schism in the broader arc of creation—though it certainly was. All that mattered, in that moment, was that it was a coming-apart for this particular family; this tribe that had grown so close on the road (in the way that any youth group that has ever piled in a tiny hot bus and set out on mission trip will affirm). Perhaps Jesus didn't know that this was *the* last meal they would all share together—but he knew it would be *one* of the last. He knew this great shifting was upon them, whether in hours or days or weeks. So he marked it with bread.

When I give the words of institution on Sunday mornings, it goes something like this: "On the night when Jesus would be betrayed, he gathered his people. And he said, 'Listen, everything is about to change. So I'm going to give you something. This bread—so that, as often as you are hungry, you will remember me. And this cup—so that, as often as you are thirsty, you will remember me. But more importantly—most importantly—remember me as often as you are together. And I will be with you.'"

With everything coming apart at the seams, there is so much more he might have given them. And in the days ahead, they would be haunted in wondering why he didn't. Why didn't he leave them an itinerary, telling them where to go next? Why didn't he leave them some secret weapon, some divine force that would keep them safe from their adversaries? Why didn't he at least tell them what that damn fig tree parable was about, or teach them that cool party trick with the water and the wine?

But he didn't. Instead, he broke the bread and he poured some wine, and he gave them to each other. He left them to each other's care. And isn't that all we need to know?

We belong to each other.

In his last spoken words from the cross, he did the same thing when he asked his best friend to take care of his mama, and his mama to feed his friend. "Woman, here is your son; friend, here is your mother." That one line . . . that one line is why I wind up a weepy hot mess on Good Friday, every single time. He gave them to each other. He gave them all to each other, and to us by extension.

The disciples gradually figure that out, in fits and starts, throughout the book of Acts. And then . . . well, life happened, and there were some letters where Paul isn't very nice to the ladies, and some stuff in Revelation that gets mishandled and taken out of context *a lot*. And then there were the Crusades, and then it's just all kind of downhill from there.

But for just a minute, with that bread held overhead in benediction, and that wine poured as a powerful reminder of how miraculous love and life together can be—Jesus gave us to each other, and asked us to remember. And so we do. Every time we gather at a table, every time we invite the new neighbor, or the newly single mom, or the newly settled refugee to come and be our people—we remember Jesus, who gave us the table. We tend our roots. And we show up. It's all we can do sometimes, but we believe it is enough.

AROUND THE TABLE:
QUESTIONS FOR DISCUSSION

1. Can you think of a time when you felt displaced? What person, place, or invitation helped you feel connected and at home?
2. What are some other stories in Scripture that model the art of neighboring?
3. Set some neighboring goals for your family: Who are people you don't know well, but would like to? Who is someone who might be feeling disconnected or discouraged?
4. How does your church practice hospitality for people (or groups of people) who may be lacking in support?

8

Forgiveness: The Daily Bread of Relationships

The process of articulating and prioritizing values—and then viewing every decision, purchase, and relationship through the lens of those values—can be a life-giving, transformative process. It can help you make major life choices, deepen connections, make for a more meaningful faith journey, and even reduce stress and anxiety.

To that end, building a life around a values system has as much to do with what you let go as what you embrace.

Maybe, for example, living out the value of abundance makes you realize how much stuff you have—so you do a big purge of possessions. This frees up space in your life (and closet); it also frees up time, because you don't spend as much time sifting through last season's castoffs to find that one thing that you always wind up wearing, no matter how much other junk is in there. You live more simply, you move more freely, you have less stuff to manage. What might that leave room for?

Perhaps the practice of nonviolence leads you to abandon a show that you used to watch regularly. Or maybe intentional acts of compassion lead you to let go of a low-boiling rage that seems to follow you everywhere (like the car line). You get the picture. Sometimes values are about adding practices. But in many cases, letting a certain moral code influence your life choices has the opposite effect. It removes the burden of that which no longer serves us.

Now, take that principle and apply it to people. The clutter that builds up, over time, in our relationships often needs to be sifted through, aired out, fluffed, and simplified.

In our marriages, with our siblings, in relation to our grown children, or maybe among our oldest friends—a lifetime of stuff can get heavy if we never learn to release old hurts and disappointments.

I'm talking about forgiveness. And it is hard work.

As a pastor, I see my share of heartbreak. It can't be oversimplified, as each person's pain is unique and each relationship complex in its own way. But there are often familiar patterns to human connection: a person is deeply wounded by a loved one. They struggle to process the world through this new lens of heartbreak. It doesn't matter if it is a sibling, a spouse, a friend, or a parent/child relationship—we are hurt most profoundly by those we love. It is, in fact, the cost of loving, and perhaps just the cost of being a person.

What I notice, often, is the *impulse of grace* that comes into most relationships at the first moment of fracture. Let's call it "the mercy instinct." The first and immediate reaction of the one who's been wounded is usually to forgive, and begin to salvage what is left of the connection.

However: the first reaction does not always win. What's so amazing is not just how easily that instinct comes—but how fiercely we fight it down when it does.

Perhaps that impulse of grace is a survival mechanism. Some well-tuned work of evolution that ensures we continue to procreate, nurture children, and live in tribes for protection. This instinct ensures that we resist ending a relationship, cutting a much loved friend/child/spouse/sibling out of our lives. And so our most natural inclination is to forgive, restore, and move on.

But then baser instincts take over. The impulse to retaliate: to hurt as we have been hurt, or to prove how right and good we are (as opposed to how wrong and bad the people who've hurt us are). And while the mercy instinct might be the quickest and the most natural, the impulses of anger, fear, and control tend to be louder and longer in duration.

Perhaps that is survival talking, too: the feeling that, if we forgive the one who has wronged us, we will be condoning their actions, and inviting another future heartbreak. Meanwhile, there is a lingering fear of guilt and shame turned inward: *If I forgive this person, really and truly . . . what wrong of mine will I have to face? Whose forgiveness will I have to seek, in order to be fully whole?* And even on our best days, we really don't want to go there. Note: This is why Hallmark does not make atonement cards to send our loved ones during Lent, Safeway does not make repentance cakes, and *Peanuts* never did a holiday special about Ash Wednesday. It's hard work, it's messy, it's complicated, and it sometimes forces us to face some inner demons that we'd rather hoped had moved on somewhere. Perhaps to a nice condo on the Gulf Coast.

Forgiveness does not come easy. Nothing worth having ever does. Nor does it always take the shape we think it ought to.

Where I come from—southeastern Kentucky—and in many other parts of the world, there resides a misguided theology of forgiveness that often compels women to stay in unhealthy, even abusive relationships. "This is just your cross to bear," they might be advised by a pastor. Or to a child who's been abused, "Christ forgave you, so you have to forgive her."

"Honor your father and mother."

"The man is the head of the household, just as Christ is the head of the Church."

They've got a million of them. But, no sir. That is not how this works.

This is not to say that every pastor from my neck of the woods would say these things to a woman or child in a bad situation; nor is this interpretation of a forgiving spirit limited to the rural South. Rather, it's rooted in a certain brand of fundamentalism; one that relies on substitutionary atonement theology, rigid gender roles, and a certain expectation that families keep up appearances when all is not well. That is a dangerous perfect storm of cultural factors.

And so, whenever I write or preach about forgiveness, I am careful to first make this one thing clear: God does not ask us to stay with people who hurt us. To "turn the other cheek" does not mean to take abuse. "Honor thy father and mother" does not mean you have to restore an adult relationship with the parent who harmed you as a child.

This is a profoundly liberating distinction for some people— that we can forgive a person in our hearts, but not have to keep them in our lives. In fact, I will never forget one woman who was visiting my congregation in Phoenix for the first time. She was a caregiver, and had brought the young women from the neighborhood group home who often attended worship with us. So, she had not even necessarily come to church on purpose this particular day. She was just doing her job.

The sermon was about forgiveness. I do not remember the text, or the liturgical season, I don't even remember if the message was any good or not. But I remember, very clearly, that one part about how forgiveness does not mean enduring abuse, or staying with people who hurt us. It was almost a casual aside, something I didn't even include in my notes. But this woman came up to me afterward, a funny look on her face. It was skepticism. It was disbelief. It was also something like a lightbulb coming on. It was something like hope.

"Hi," she said, balancing a cup of coffee in one hand, watching her charges out of the corner of her eye. (They had cookies. They weren't going anywhere.) "What you said earlier . . . about forgiveness. You're saying . . . well, I can forgive someone, but that doesn't mean I have to stay with them?" She said this in the way that you say something you believe is too good to be true. Something you are a little afraid to hope for.

In that moment I got one of those Holy Spirit taps on the shoulder that says, "This is important. Pay attention. Show up. Be in this moment as hard and fast as you know how."

"Yes," I said, looking her in the eye. I wanted to grab her by both shoulders and say, "Is he hurting you? There is help!"

Instead, I just said again, "Yes. Forgiveness can be healing for a relationship. But sometimes it can just be healing for your spirit. You can forgive and move on, and *you don't have to stay with someone who hurts you.*"

"I've never heard anybody say that before," she said, near tears. "Thank you."

I never saw her again. But that Holy Spirit, chill down the spine, *show up and say this one thing* moment gives me great hope that she got out of whatever it was. Or away from whomever it was.

I'll say it again. Forgiveness is a matter of the Spirit. Sometimes you forgive and move forward, together; sometimes, you forgive and move on, in new freedom. God does not ask us to stay in places where we're being hurt.

PRACTICING FORGIVENESS AT HOME

While it is true that forgiveness is a spiritual matter, and can be accomplished outside of the personal connection, it is also true that, sometimes, we give up far too easily on people we love. We bail because it's easier than powering through the discomfort; easier than feeling the pain of betrayal; easier than giving up our pride.

I'm talking about: elderly brothers who go to their graves having not spoken in 40 years—*25 of which* they spent having forgotten what they were mad about; friends who drift as life changes, and then spend decades, each mad at the other, for not having called; children who spoke harshly to parents in a moment of anger, and parents who cling to the blow as a backward way of staying connected to the child; or the congregation that cannot—to save its own life—let go of the hurts of 20 years ago and move the heck on, for Christ's sake. I'm not taking the Lord's name in vain . . . I literally mean, for Christ's sake, churches have to learn to let go of that decades-old conflict—or perhaps just an outmoded notion of who they were supposed to be—and move on in new life.

Forgiveness is daily bread. Not because of a particular theology of the Communion Table and the grace it extends—but because forgiveness and mercy are things we extend to our loved ones daily. Sometimes for nothing much—the shoes left on the floor for the 800th time, when our spouse has asked us, twice daily for 12 years, to pick them up (guilty). Or the snappish tone over nothing in particular that escalated into an "I don't know what we're fighting about but I realize I am mad about many other inconsequential things right now" moment.

Of course, sometimes we need forgiveness to cover the depths of a much larger chasm. But however great or small the pain itself, the practice of letting go of resentment is a critical daily practice. Think again of a purge of possessions: you can move intentionally through the house about once a week or once a month, getting rid of the junk that's accumulated; and then maybe once a season go through and do a bigger sweep of what's been outgrown or broken or is no longer needed. It's not such an overwhelming task and you always feel reasonably in control of your space. But go help someone move who has lived in their house for 30 years without ever really noticing what's piling up in the attic, the basement, the garage, the linen closet . . . You find yourself faced with a seemingly insurmountable task that is not just physical, but deeply emotional. I've often heard people joke that it would not be the worst thing if the whole house burned down (*ha ha, nervous laughter*). "If it weren't for the pictures" they would just let the whole thing go rather than do the work of discernment and self-examination that comes with having to let go.

The same is true of our relationships. We can let "junk" build up over a lifetime. Little resentments over nothing major, maybe a few hurts that run deeper but never exactly broke us. Before we know it, all that stuff has taken up residence in our souls, and after a certain point, we find it's easier to just let it burn . . . maybe sever the connection entirely rather than have to confront so many complicated and hurtful dimensions of this life together.

This daily practice of letting go is perhaps the most critical in marriage. If we live long enough, marriage can be our longest-enduring human relationship. We live with our spouse far longer than we live as children with our parents, and longer than our children live with us; and longer than we live at home with our siblings. Specifically, because it is the longest-enduring, in-house relationship, marriage has the most potential for the epic *piling up of stuff* that can lead to some pretty heavy resentment, if we don't shake it out on a regular basis.

You've heard it said, "Do not go to bed angry at your spouse." But verily, I say unto you, that is bananas. If you are up late in a fight with your spouse, chances are that 80 percent of the emotion in the room is related to fatigue and irritability. Go to bed. Sleep. It is possible that you might wake up in the morning still feeling mildly annoyed, but having mostly forgotten what all the drama was for. At the same time, it is important to communicate, articulate, and process the shared life daily, so that its tensions don't grow into major fractures in the retaining wall. This is daily bread—the pattern of release-and-connect that makes it possible to live in proximity with another person.

One daily bread practice that I've learned is to have a "One Thing." Or maybe several One Things. What I always tell couples in premarital counseling is, there may be days that it's hard to be together. Find one thing about your spouse—something they did for you, something they gave up for you, something extraordinary about them that you really love, or maybe just a trait you find especially endearing—put that One Thing in some kind of emotional file folder. And when you, from time to time, find your partner to be *the most infuriating person on the planet*, go to that file and pull out your One Thing. Maybe you've got a few of those things, for an especially rough day. It's amazing how many everyday resentments can be warded off by practicing this kind of grace.

Daily bread.

One of the "one things" in my marriage has always been my husband's support for my career. When we first met, I had just started seminary and had little idea what it would mean for my life. He had even less an idea what it would mean for his life. (I'm talking date number one here.) But one of the first conversations of substance that we had was my struggle with some close, lifelong friends who could not accept me going to seminary. And he, this guy I had just met (kind of randomly, in the housekeeping area of the hotel where we both worked), was incensed on my behalf. Knowing little about the career path itself, he was fiercely determined that if I wanted to, I should do this thing.

That, I thought on date number one, is a good man.

And so he is. And has been, as he stood by me (literally) at my ordination; as we've moved twice across the country for my jobs. As he decided to leave work and stay home with our kids when two babies and a church *and* a hotel, which he managed, turned out to be too much for one family to manage. He's not an especially churchy guy himself, but he has played in praise bands, learned the art of vetting a sermon, and mastered the potluck. Ministry makes for a full and beautiful life but I'm not gonna lie; it's also a weird one. Ask anybody. And that my husband—who had never known or heard of a woman pastor before meeting me—has conceded to build much of his life around this calling of mine . . . well, let's just say that goes a long way when he's yelling at me to pick up my shoes (again), or when the strain of moving and parenting small children makes us snappish.

I do not, in any universe, pretend to have the perfect marriage, or to have mastered some carefully choreographed relationship dynamics that would work in every relationship. Marriage is an art, not a science, and there is no one magic formula that will make it always work.

But I will say—without judgment upon those whose marriages didn't work out, and with no shame for those who decided the most life-giving thing for all was to move on—a marriage sustained by the daily bread of intentional grace is one more likely to endure.

The practice of extending these daily small mercies will reach beyond marriage and into our other relationships. It will be modeled for our kids; it will inform our relationships with our siblings and parents. It will shape the way we navigate the evolving relationship with adult children, and perhaps their children.

That first impulse toward grace and forward motion is the best, truest, and most Spirit-filled way ahead—not just to restored connection but to a self that we can live with. That does not mean trust comes back easily, nor does it mean that all is forgotten. But it does say: *I love you more than this moment. You are more than this wrong. There is more to our story than either of us can see right now. This connection, to me, is worth enduring an element of heartbreak.*

The mercy instinct is a good one, and one that, we must believe, was placed there at creation by the God in whose image we were born. The impulse of grace is survival itself; for our families, and for the world.

Sometimes, forgiveness is just for the good of our own souls. For the breathing room that appears when we let go of some hurt, some burden we hauled around too long thinking it would somehow punish the one who harmed us (it won't). Even if we have done a good job of practicing daily forgiveness, and clearing out the clutter of our relationships as we go, most everyone has someone they need to forgive. And everyone has something for which they need to be forgiven.

This may take a lifetime of spiritual, emotional, and physical work to reckon with. But sometimes, naming the person or experience that burdens us can give us a fresh perspective, or a renewed energy for healing and reconnection. Sometimes, we just have to make like a Disney princess and "let it go."

PRACTICING FORGIVENESS IN COMMUNITY

In a perfect world, the faith community supports and restores us for the work of forgiveness and healing in our own relationships. But the community can also enact the mercy impulse on the world. And when that happens, it reveals the grace of God in powerful ways.

The unfortunate literature I encountered in Amish country notwithstanding, this is a faith tradition that has deeply explored and embodied the concept of grace. In 2006, a gunman in Nickel Mines, Pennsylvania, shot ten girls in a one-room schoolhouse. Five of them died, while the others were seriously wounded. The 32-year-old shooter then took his own life.

The same day, that Amish community issued a statement of forgiveness to the shooter's family. The media didn't know what to make of it. The general public was shocked—possibly even a little offended. How could these families, who had just endured such a horrific loss at the hands of a monster, possibly be talking about forgiveness? It did not add up. At least, not with what most people think about how the mercy instinct is supposed to work. Doesn't there first have to be some act of contrition on the part of the wrongdoer? Or, barring that, at least a significant passage of time since the transgression?

But the Amish way rejects those cultural assumptions. The book *Amish Grace* mines the seeming disconnect between the tragic events of that day and the story that unfolded. Eventually, the faithful response of the community became the dominant narrative in the public eye; which, ultimately, transformed the act of violence into a story of mercy. The story was adapted for film as well. This passage from the book highlights the power of forgiveness to transform the world beyond our own interactions:

> Running against [the mainstream] grain, finding alternative ways to imagine our world, ways that in turn facilitate forgiveness, takes more than individual willpower. We are not only the products of our culture, we are also producers of our culture. We need to construct cultures that value and nurture forgiveness. In their own way, the Amish have constructed such an environment. The challenge for the rest of us is to use our resources creatively to shape cultures that discourage revenge as a first response. How might we work more imaginatively to create communities in which enemies are treated as members of the human family and not demonized? How might these communities foster visions

that enable their members to see offenders, as well as victims, as persons with authentic needs?[1]

A similar countercultural response came in the aftermath of a church shooting in Charleston. The self-proclaimed white supremacist, who murdered nine people at Mother Emmanuel AME, said in a statement that he had hoped to provoke a race war in the South. But that isn't what he got. What he did witness—and, more importantly, what the city of Charleston witnessed—was some of the survivors, and victims' families, and church leaders speaking "the language of forgiveness," as noted in the *Time* magazine piece that warranted a place on the cover.[2] There followed public demonstrations of interracial unity all over the city, even around the country. And it was the sentiment of grace and solidarity—not the hateful act itself—that spurred meaningful conversations about removing the Confederate flag from government buildings in South Carolina.

These stories demonstrate some of the deepest kinds of loss and pain we can imagine. But they also demonstrate the transformative witness of the gospel when it is embodied and enacted. The faith communities in these stories exercised Jesus' Third Way of relationship with an oppressor. The mercy extended in the wake of a terrible crime did not emerge out of a vacuum, nor by accident. The principle of forgiveness lies at the heart of the values practiced in their shared life of faith, so that, in a moment of crisis, it comes bubbling up to the surface as the instinctive response to evil.

Too often, we carry around that which harms us as though the weight of it will somehow punish the other. But the Gospels model turning other cheek; not in a way that leaves us victims, but in a way that empowers us for relationship, and for the work of good news in the world. We can cultivate that instinct toward mercy—in prayer, in practice, and in the life of community—so that our first instinct is always the best one.

In the meantime, I pray for a day when our stories of transformation don't so often begin with violence.

FORGIVENESS IN SCRIPTURE

Either Jesus was a man of few words, or else the disciples were rotten note takers. We don't have much documentation of things he actually said. We do have four different versions of the few things he might have said, and the bulk of it is stories—those about Jesus and those Jesus told.

In every church I've ever served there has been one guy who has this certain way about him in meetings. He doesn't say much. He listens well. And at some point—usually around the end of the meeting—this guy will say something pretty short and concise that is *exactly the right thing to say.* It is as though he's managed to process an hour-long (or three-hours long) conversation into a few short sentences, find the right note to wrap up on, and generally leave us with a great spark of wisdom and even a next step. I'd like to learn to be that guy. But alas, I am a talker.

I'm pretty sure Jesus was *that guy.* He didn't say much, but when he did speak, what he said was exactly the right thing. And everyone felt heard and valued, and it was wise and it was good and it gave the people a way forward. Even if it wasn't the one they wanted or expected, it was a good way.

So when Jesus gives a brief instruction on prayer, we ought to especially sit up and pay attention. He doesn't say much—and even less of what he says is direct instruction. But here is a rare glimpse of him in an actual didactic situation. His model prayer:

> "When you are praying, do not heap up empty phrases as the Gentiles do; for they think that they will be heard because of their many words. Do not be like them, for your Father knows what you need before you ask him.
> "Pray then in this way:
>
> Our Father in heaven,
> hallowed be your name.
> Your kingdom come.
> Your will is done, on earth as it is in heaven.
> Give us this day our daily bread.
> And forgive us our debts,
> As we also have forgiven our debtors.

And do not bring us to the time of trial,
but rescue us from the evil one.

*"For if you forgive others their trespasses, your heavenly Father
will also forgive you; but if you do not forgive others, neither
will your Father forgive your sins."*
(Matt. 6:7–15, italics added)

Aside from the greeting and the signing-off part, this prayer
only asks for five things:

1. That God's name be made known and be made holy
2. That God's will be known on earth, as it is in the divine
   realm
3. That the people be fed
4. That we be forgiven and learn to forgive.
5. That we be protected from evil; the evil of the world, and
   that which might be, shall we say, self-directed

That's a pretty short list. And two of its decidedly few items
have to do with forgiveness. That's a pretty strong clue that
forgiveness is *important;* for our own spiritual health, for the
depth of our relationships, and for the good of the world.

Also significant: that *this is a two-fold forgiveness.* It is not
enough to ask God's forgiveness but not extend that same grace
to our neighbor; nor is it sufficient to forgive one who hurt us,
while failing to seek God's mercy on our own failings. The two
exercises are linked, and cannot be extracted from each other.

Notice also that Jesus' prayer asks for daily bread; we can
assume, then, that the nature of this prayer is that of a daily discipline. The psalms are full of prayers for special occasions—
profound lament, rage, grief; celebration, thanksgiving, praise;
in fact, those prayers go on for a bit. There is a psalm for everything and some of them are not so short.

Jesus' prayer, on the other hand, is the prayer of ritual; a liturgy
for every ordinary day; words that draw the holy into our everyday
routine, transforming common tasks into something sacred.

Forgiveness, then, is not a special occasion prayer. It is not
the practice you put in your back pocket and save until the

wheels come off, the bottom drops out, and the world is on fire. There are psalms for that. This is the prayer of the everyday sacred. *And forgiveness is needed in that daily rhythm, every bit as much as bread.*

It is a bit of a bummer that this is one of the only prayers we hear Jesus pray. I would imagine he gave some epic table graces. Like before he did that trick with the wine. Or when he met the fellas on the beach after he came back from the dead. Or right before he did that thing with the pigs to send the demon over a cliff. That is some powerful prayer. But we don't hear those. Instead, we get these words of everyday blessing; the practice of forgiveness that ties us to our people daily, and to the rest of the world, if we do it right.

One of the few other times we do hear Jesus pray is from the cross. Through the greatest suffering imaginable he says, "Father, forgive them . . . they know not what they do." Mercy like that—extended to others in a moment of great pain—does not just happen. Nor can the depth of that mercy be strictly spoken. It comes from a life of deep prayer and intention; from the practices of everyday faith, shared in community; and from the daily grace of letting go, so that we can better love the world.

AROUND THE TABLE:
QUESTIONS FOR DISCUSSION

1. When you have conflict, does your focus go first to what the other person has done or what you have done?
2. Think about people you might need to forgive: someone from whom you've been estranged, someone from whom you might become estranged if you don't forgive, someone who needs to stay out of your life, maybe someone you don't even know in person. Were you surprised by any of the people who came to mind?
3. Which is harder: forgiving others, or forgiving ourselves?
4. What are some everyday ways that we can practice forgiveness, letting go, and moving on?

9

Equality: Made in God's Image

The small boys were screaming—nay, shrieking—on the playground. It was all in good 4-year-old fun, but dang, it was shrill. It was headache-inducing. Anyone with ears would have wanted it to stop.

Including the dad who finally approached them. "Oh good," I thought. "Adult intervention!" But then I overheard this exchange:

"Hey," he said, "hey, cut it out. Are you boys? *Or are you little girls?*"

Oh, *hell* no. He did *not* just do that.

But yes, he sure did. And you know what? *It worked.* They stopped their shrieking banshee efforts on a dime. Quicker than children that age can usually be persuaded with ice cream, Pixar, or the threat of punishment. All it took was that simple question: *Are you boys, or are you girls?*

Because in our world, the worst thing you can call someone is a girl. It is the most profound insult you can sling at the male of the species, regardless of their age or stature. Even a 4-year-old boy picks up on the implied undesirable nature of being perceived as feminine. That aversion sticks, through the

adolescent years, and affects not only the ways that boys inter-
act with women, but also how they see themselves; and how
they react to other boys who may be perceived as less "manly,"
for whatever reason. These acts of disparaging of the feminine,
in the broad sense, lay the foundations of many social ills—
including sexual harassment, homophobia, and bullying.

I'm sure that this dad—who took time out of his day to
volunteer at his kid's preschool—is probably not an uber-
sexist Neanderthal type. And yet, he made this off-hand com-
ment like it was nothing. As if there were not *actual* little girls
nearby—playing happily and *not* screaming, and just beginning to learn that being a girl is viewed by many as some sort of
punishment or handicap that God dealt them at birth.

I've always considered myself a feminist, but I didn't truly
start to hear conversations like these for what they were until
I had a daughter. And now that I have a son, I am even more
attuned to these microaggressions towards women, in all their
subtle and not-so-subtle expressions. From the dad on the playground, gently chiding the boys for acting like girls; to the dad
in the grocery store, wearing a "Playboy Talent Scout" T-shirt
as his wife and young daughter followed behind.

You don't have to be a parent to wake up to the kinds of
language, behaviors, and corporate practices that add up to
misogynistic messaging. And the scope of prejudice, inherent
in such instances, is not just limited to anti-woman sentiment.
The overarching message is one of disdain for anything that is
not distinctly masculine, in the most traditional sense of the
word. The message of "why would anyone want to be a girl?"
is firmly rooted in much of the homophobic and transphobic
culture that can make life so painful and difficult for gender
non-conforming people, especially children and youth.

Having children and trying to raise them with an inclusive worldview has given me a fresh perspective on my own
life experience. It is worth noting that I am a straight, white
woman. I'm educated, I've been afforded a great deal of opportunity in a male-dominated field, and I've always had support
at home—from my parents, as a child, and, more recently,

from my husband—for any interest I've wanted to pursue. And yet—even with all this privilege and relative security—I can glance back over my life and see four decades of microaggression toward women, encapsulated in my own limited experience. From the subtle forms, like the junior high math teacher who made special Barbie-related illustrations so the girls could understand what he was talking about; to the less subtle, like funeral directors who accost me before a service and tell me I have no business being a pastor. All the while encroaching on my personal space.

I have a list of these encounters, from the micro to the in-your-face, a mile long. If you are a woman, you've got your own running list, and chances are it puts mine to shame. If you are gay or lesbian or bisexual or trans or a person of color, then I am certain your list puts mine to shame. Our society has been failing to truly value equality since the moment it first claimed to. "All men are created equal"? Even that was disingenuous, ignoring the existence of enslaved black men, not to mention women and all other minorities.

As far as we have come in the way of gender equality since then, we still live with some harmful prejudices about gender and sexuality that are in direct conflict with the inclusive nature of the gospel. Ironically, those often-harmful gender norms are enforced, in large part, by Christian churches upholding those values as gospel, rather than the secular cultural norms that they are.

The heteronormative one man–one woman model of partnership is one of the hallmarks of the traditional family values movement. More conservative expressions of the Church have been the ones leading the charge in movements that limit the rights of transgender people. And political candidates that stake their platform on antiwoman and antigay rhetoric are nearly always backed by high-profile religious leaders.

When these voices dominate the conversation, the damage is far-reaching. Such short-sightedness is harmful to individuals and family connections; harmful to the community of faith that continues to be torn apart, as it dwells in issues at the expense of compassion; it is even harmful to future generations of the faithful, who will be working for years to overcome the ill effects of this rigid dialogue.

Former President Jimmy Carter wrote an essay, and then a book, on his struggle with gender oppression within the church of his upbringing, and his ultimate decision to leave. He notes:

> At its most repugnant, the belief that women must be subjugated to the wishes of men excuses slavery, violence, forced prostitution, genital mutilation and national laws that omit rape as a crime. But it also costs many millions of girls and women control over their own bodies and lives, and continues to deny them fair access to education, health, employment and influence within their own communities.
>
> The impact of these religious beliefs touches every aspect of our lives. They help explain why in many countries boys are educated before girls; why girls are told when and whom they must marry; and why many face enormous and unacceptable risks in pregnancy and childbirth because their basic health needs are not met. . . .
>
> The same discriminatory thinking lies behind the continuing gender gap in pay and why there are still so few women in office in the West. The root of this prejudice lies deep in our histories, but its impact is felt every day. It is not women and girls alone who suffer. It damages all of us.[1]

Indeed, the crimes committed against women all over the world—from the microaggressions I experience in my relatively comfortable life, to chronic, systemic violence—does damage to men and women alike. And damages the dignity of the created world and God's intended life for its inhabitants.

When the Duggar family—made popular by their reality show *19 Kids and Counting*—found themselves in the spotlight for incidents of sexual abuse, they dealt with it by calling it anything but that. Rather it was "a youthful indiscretion"; "a series of inappropriate behaviors"; evidence that "we are not a perfect family." But the news that the oldest son, Josh (then 27) had, as a teenager, repeatedly molested and sexually assaulted his younger sisters and another unnamed minor was beyond "inappropriate." It was, and is, a crime. And one for which no charges were pressed, given the three-year statute of limitations in the state of Arkansas, as well as many other states. This is the sort of harm that can come of systemic fundamentalism—the kind that limits the role of women to that of wife and mother; the kind that prohibits women from leading and teaching in the faith community; the kind that constantly reminds women they are a class set apart and less-than.

Not all conservatism is synonymous with abusive behavior. But conservative doctrine can manifest in toxic systems of fundamentalism that allow for—even condone—systemic abuse. The costs of fundamentalism—whether in Christianity, Islam, or a secular cult with violent tendencies—are far-reaching, and not just detrimental to women. Fundamentalism is how Waco happened. Fundamentalism is how ISIS continues to gain traction at an alarming rate.

Fundamentalism is why so many people, male and female alike, have horrific stories of being abused as children by Catholic priests.

When the incident with the Duggar family came to light, the immediate concern was not for the victims but for the moral purity of the young man. In public statements, the father indicated that they had dealt with the matter as a family, and had taken it to the elders of their church. Police were informed, but no formal charges were filed. There was no continuing investigation. The story, as it appeared in the news, never seemed to be about the crime. It was primarily about how the family was "reeling" from the public disclosure; and how Josh Duggar would not be able to continue his career as the professional face of "family values."

This family was in the spotlight for this scandal because they were already in the spotlight—as the embodiment of "family values" no less. But it's not just about them. This one instance (or this one perpetrator) reflects the heart of a certain kind of fundamentalism that privileges heterosexual men over all other expressions of God's image. Whether the group in question is Christian, Muslim, or a secular cult with a self-proclaimed prophet and a series of doomsday billboards along the highway, it all amounts to the same fear and silence; the same cost to human dignity.

PRACTICING EQUALITY AT HOME

In recent years, there's been a productive movement to cull the "r" word (retarded) from our cultural vocabulary, because it is hurtful to actual people with special needs. We've also made significant strides in eliminating "gay" as a negative adjective. So why do we still just accept it when otherwise kind and intelligent people sling "girl" around as the ultimate existential defeat?

It's not just dads on playgrounds. It's coaches on football fields. "You guys are playing like a bunch of girls!" Except they are more likely, in those cases, to use crass euphemisms for female genitalia. Which is ironic, considering how most of them entered the world.

It's CEOs saying "man up," when what they mean is "step up and lead." It's churches urging their men to "be men," implying that they need to be more authoritative within their family. Wear the pants and all that. It's the father watching in horror as his small son playfully tries on a pair of pink shoes. "*Not my boy*," he bellows angrily, while his daughter wonders, "What's wrong with my shoes? I wear those all the time." And while other kids, made to wear blue and play football when they really want to wear pink and do ballet, wonder if they'll ever be seen and accepted for who they truly are.

A thousand little jokes every day make their way into our collective psyches, through the airwaves, the newsfeed, the buffoon in the cubicle next door, or maybe even the well-meaning dad on the playground. It starts right there.

Harmless, most people would say. A joke. The natural order of things. And yet . . . women still make 77 cents on the dollar. Women are still grossly underrepresented in every sector of public leadership. And *one in four* American women—this number has not changed since the first heart-stopping time I heard it—one in *four* will be sexually assaulted in her lifetime. Furthermore, thirty-two states still do not have laws in place to protect against discrimination based on sexual orientation. LGB and Questioning youth are four times more likely to attempt suicide than their peers, and nearly half of transgender youth have seriously contemplated suicide—a full quarter having attempted it.[2]

That starts on the playground. And it runs deep.

Perhaps the first step in how we train up our children in a more life-affirming way is to stop telling boys in these subtle and not-so-subtle ways that a girl is the worst thing they could possibly be, that they are somehow "less than" if they do not excel at sports or stifle every tear that comes to their eyes. And stop telling girls that being a girl is a limitation, that she can only succeed in certain fields and needs to tone down her personality to be taken seriously.

"Girl" is not a synonym for weak, slow, loud, pushy, hard to please, unreasonable, cowardly, mean, or underachieving.

Look at all those words. All those words that we call girls, every single day.

But all those words can mean exactly what they say. All by themselves, with no analogy. If someone is being loud or pushy, tell them they're being loud or pushy. If somebody is moving too slow (driving like a girl) or acting weak (throwing like a girl), then just *use the words* "slow" and "weak." It's just that simple.

Words are not the only thing. But words do matter. Every single day, in every place from the playground on, words matter very much.

Giving kids the language to empower themselves, and each other, is an important part of helping them understand the full personhood of every human being—male or female, gay or straight, transgender or cis.

Beyond words, we also seek to model for our kids, boys and girls alike, that regardless of gender or sexual orientation, all people are gifted in important and unique ways, and all people are called to demonstrate dignity, grace, and compassion, in the image of God.

I love basketball, though I was never very good at it. I was short. I was slow. But moreover—I was easily intimidated by (a) faster kids and (b) fast-moving objects flying at my face.

I have a girl child, however, who is neither short nor slow. She's this long-legged thing (like her dad) and she can sprint. She is tall and fast, in other words, unlike me as a kid. And as for the easily intimidated part . . . well, we are working on it.

To this end, coed sports are the best and worst thing ever. It's the best because, in theory, kids at this young age are just learning team spirit and cooperation, and those are things that kids need to learn in cross-gender situations. It's the worst because already, at a young age, the boys have picked up on the memo that *you don't want to pass the ball to a girl if you can help it.*

Seriously, they are 7. Where do they get this? I'm starting to think it is deeply engrained in the womb, and then reinforced in a thousand small ways from the minute they are born.

Case in point: At Target the other day, an employee saw my 5-year-old boy trip and fall. "Are you OK, buddy?" he asked. Which was very sweet. "Do you need a Band-Aid or something?" Also sweet. But he wasn't done. "Do you need a Band-Aid . . . or are you a man?"

No, I didn't get all feminist Mama Bear at this kid in Target—who was really just trying to be helpful—but are you telling me that now, men are so tough they *literally do not bleed*? Because that's what I'm hearing, bro. If you admit it hurts, you aren't a man. If you need a Band-Aid, you might as well be a *girl*. And we know that is the worst thing you can be, ever.

That seemed to be the message the boys at my daughter's coed basketball camp had received. There were only two girls, and the rest were boys. The girls were really good. Mine, long and tall and a great sprinter, with good defensive instincts. The other, little but scrappy, and an excellent shot.

And yet the boys acted like they weren't even there.

There was one kid, in particular (isn't there always That One Kid?) who, no matter what else was going on, would be waving his arms like a maniac yelling "Pass! Pass!" To be fair, it might not have been gender-driven for him—he was an equal opportunity ball hog. He didn't want anyone else to touch the ball, ever. Even when the coach was holding the ball and talking, this kid was all up in his face with hands out, like "gimmeit, gimmeit, gimmeit."

Several times, I witnessed my giraffe of a girl make a bold steal. And the minute she got her hands on the ball—every time—That One Kid would shout, "Pass! Pass!" And she passed it, every time. Handed it over like she was holding something hot.

The (male) coach finally, thankfully, pulled her aside one day and said, "*You* keep the ball. Look, you can dribble *all the way up here* to the net and shoot. You get the ball, you shoot it yourself."

"Great job," I said when she came over for a water break. "Listen, did you hear what Coach said? *You do not have to pass the ball just because a boy tells you to pass the ball.*"

"But I'm not a very good shooter," she says.

And I'm all, "That's not true! You just aren't getting a chance!" Then I got reinforcements from the mom next to me. "You can do it!" she says to my kid, whose name she doesn't even know.

It really does take a village.

I have no idea if my kid is going to be an athlete. She also loves ballet. And writing stories. She's also an artist. And a vegetarian/animal lover who wants to be a vet, or an environmental activist. She also loves church, and talks about preaching a lot. Lord help me, she might be a minister. This is not about basketball. This is about early lessons in gender politics; early reminders to stand up for yourself; and to not be afraid of the stuff flying at your face. She may not be an athlete. But if she's not, it won't be for lack of height or speed. And on my watch, it will sure as hell never, ever be because she's intimidated.

Also, on my watch, I am trying to raise a son who will never be That One Kid—the one who shouts for the girl to "pass" and let the boys do the hard part. I want him to be a feminist, like so many good men that I know: men who understand that you don't have to be a woman to think women are whole people, deserving of equal pay, equal respect, and equal authority in the world. I do not have any right way or one way to make that happen, but it has a lot to do with language we use; and language we don't use. It also has to do with teaching him personal space (which, as a naturally cuddly koala bear of a kid, he struggles with mightily). As he gets a little older, those conversations about personal space can evolve into discussions about consent; ground zero in talking about rape culture.

It starts here. At 2, 4, 6 years old, our children are being conditioned for a binary blue/pink world. The shows they watch, the books they read, the language on the playground—even the toy aisles at Target, which are divided into *pink everything* and everything else—all contribute to a profoundly segregated climate. On the surface, some of these distinctions are harmless. But underneath, layers of subtle messages about belonging and empowerment are deeply destructive—to men and women alike.

Far beyond the pink Lego aisle, there are endless benefits to understanding that all people—men and women, L, G, B, T, or Q—are created in the image of God. A working vocabulary of equality provides the roots of healthy body image; the beginnings of good relationship boundaries; and a deeper sense of the holiness present in all things. Not to mention a safe climate in which kids feel they can talk about sexuality, without shame or fear of rejection.

On a side note, seriously, the girl Legos and boy Legos are in *separate aisles*. What would happen if the pink Legos touch the Star Wars Legos? What happens if a boy wants to play with the dinosaur Legos *and the princess Legos together*? I'm pretty certain the universe would implode upon itself.

PRACTICING EQUALITY IN COMMUNITY

When it comes to the harmful gender dialogue that relegates girls to second-class citizens, tells boys they have to be "tough," and puts the LGBT community in a place of perpetual "otherness," there is good news and bad news. The bad news is, much of that harmful worldview is rooted in the Church and its hyper-masculine narrative. The good news is, the faith community also has great power to reshape that narrative and reclaim the embodied dignity of men, women, and people all across the spectrum of gender identity.

The simplest and yet most profound impact we can have in building an equality worldview for our children is to model gender diversity in leadership. While I could write a book on the matter—as could many colleagues I am privileged to know—I'm not going to insert an apologetic here as to "why women should be allowed to preach." The very tone of that, "allowed," implies that we women still have to somehow answer for our presence here. And anyway, we don't have time for that. I figure if you are a person who deeply believes that women shouldn't preach, I'm probably not going to change your mind in a few paragraphs. Not to mention, if that is your belief, you probably wouldn't have bought this book. If you do still struggle to accept women in full expression of church leadership—or if you're part of a community that still experiences tension around this topic—I suggest reading Jimmy Carter's *Losing My Religion for Equality*, as well as Sarah Bessey's *Jesus Feminist*.

Meanwhile, for the rest of us, it is good for children and youth to see a diverse group of people in church leadership. If not on the paid staff, then hopefully among your worship leaders, elders, and Bible study leaders to round out young (and old) people's understanding of an embodied gospel.

Beware also the dynamic of having mostly or only women in the role of Sunday school teachers and children's worship leaders. Rooted in the days when that was *all* women could do in the church, it has become a hard-to-break cycle in even more progressive churches, and poses its own sort of problem. I worry that young boys pick up the subconscious notion that "church is for girls," and will therefore be out the door the minute they grow up. In much the same way, many of our schools still use the language of "room mom," "Den Mother," and other gender-specific language that implies that only women have been endowed with gifts for planning Halloween parties and organizing the craft table. Of course, I see dads at my kids' school every day, getting more involved than these titles would indicate. But the language still normalizes the notion that volunteering at school is mostly a mom zone. Which not only pigeonholes the mothers, but also overlooks the significant gifts that men bring to the school community.

The faith community can fall into the same traps, but a little bit of intention can go a long way. However we order worship and Christian education programs, the goal is that the diverse gifts of the community are truly represented, so that children can see themselves, however they identify, in a variety of roles and voices.

Beyond the words that we use to talk about people in various kinds of leadership, we can also be more intentional about the words we use to talk about God.

We need a more diverse lexicon for speaking about the Holy. "Father," "King," and the capital He/Him/His thing is just not cutting it. The move toward more gender neutral, or at least, gender-balanced ways of referring to God has been rejected out of hand, dismissed in many circles as politically correct, all-things-to-all-people kind of nonsense. But that is oversimplifying millennia of subtle messaging that has contributed to the disempowerment of women.

It's not just churchy circles that are trying to strike some balance when it comes to the pronouns and descriptive terms that we use. The word "mankind," for instance, has been swapped out for "humankind" in mainstream, secular speech. In academia, standards of inclusion are not just a suggestion, but an expectation; one that is part of the education itself.

Old habits die hard though. Sometimes, Scripture is what it is. It's not the end of the world if an elder says "Father God" in the Communion prayer. In the Lord's Prayer, the Doxology, and in any other number of places, "Father" just rolls right off the tongue, and there are some good old hymns that center around God as "King" that, for all our best efforts toward neutrality, just lose something in translation when we try too hard.

I've been in churches that intentionally swapped every rote "Father" with Creator; I've known others to just balance with the occasional "Mother," as well. There's no one right way, and it doesn't have to be all or nothing. But as we begin to chip away at the patriarchal language on which the Church—and much of Western Christendom—has built itself, we can see the many ways that exploring feminine expressions of God can be transformative for the faith of all people—men and women alike.

Just as important as the words we speak, though, is the kind of space we create. The conversation about LGBTQ equality in the life of the church is going to be viewed, through the lens of history, as one of the most formative issues of our time. And, many modern-day church leaders believe, the ones who stand dogmatically opposed to the full inclusion of all people will someday be viewed with the same ire as those who opposed integration or women's suffrage in the generations before us.

Institutional religion (and the values upheld by that institution) has done great harm to women, and to gender-nonconforming populations, for centuries. That is why the modern-day church is called, not just to passively welcome these groups now, but to overtly affirm their full humanness and blessedness as whole people created in God's image. In the past decade or so, I've served three different congregations that engaged this work of affirmation, each in their own unique way.

The church that I serve now, because of its reputation for being inclusive, has become a safe place for families of transgender youth and children. A core group has started a ministry to provide community and connection for parents of children (of all ages) who are in transition. The group has been contacted by the local children's hospital—which is nationally renowned for its gender transition support programs—about working in partnership with them, so that they can refer families to us who are in need of this type of care.

The group, aptly named "Transforming Families," is lay led. While faith based, it is designed to reach a population that is not specifically looking for a "Christian" study group. Even so, the community they are forming within the wider community of the church is full of Christ's love and mercy. In a time when others around us are still fighting about who should use what bathroom, a safe place that embraces the full humanity of all people, beyond embodied expressions of gender, can be the most transformative place of all.

EQUALITY IN SCRIPTURE

In the beginning. I'm as surprised as anyone that I've referred to Genesis so often in this book. But the more I think about relationships, values, and connectedness, the more I find myself there, back in the beginning of the story of God and humanity.

The first chapters of Genesis offer not one, but two creation stories. Most people who consider themselves "churched" know both stories, but if asked to tell the story of Creation, they would use elements of the two interchangeably. I know I do.

But one distinguishing factor of that first story is the language that God uses in creating the first people. "Let us create them in our image," God says. "Them" and "our" are critical here. "Them" shows that both Adam and Eve sprang from the same desire to craft human life; at the same time, in the same fashion, and for the same purpose. The two were created, equal and side by side, for the work of populating and caring for creation. It's almost as if the masculine and the feminine emerge as one creation.[3]

As for the second story, it can be helpful to look at some of the original Hebrew language in this context.

[The] English translation says that the LORD God creates "man from the dust of the ground." But in the Hebrew, *ha-'adam* is created from *ha-'adamah*. *Ha-'adamah* means earth or dirt. Thus, the LORD God uses dirt to create a dirt-being, or earthling, if you will.

The fact that we have chosen to call this first being "Adam," translate *ha-'adam* as "man," and use male pronouns, gives the impression that it was male. But it is not until the second human is created in Genesis 2:22 that the Hebrew storyline uses words for male and female. When there is only one, it is a generic human. . . . Once there are two humans, the idea of male- and femaleness is introduced. In other words, we have reason to stop saying that "Man was created first, and then Woman from his rib."

. . .

One translation of Genesis 2:18 (NRSV) says, "Then the LORD God said, 'It is not good that the human should be alone; I will make him a helper as his partner.'" For many people, [helper] means "subordinate" or "servant," suggesting that woman was made for man's benefit, in order to complete him. What we see, if we look at the Hebrew terms, however, is a bit more of a partner-on-equal-grounds idea.[4]

The Genesis story is often employed in defense of traditional gender roles. In light of this reading, however, it could just as well serve as an apologetic for gender equality; and possibly even gender *neutrality*, thus reinforcing the rights of even more suppressed populations.

The book of Proverbs also features an interesting feminine character, first known as Sophia, or "Woman Wisdom," as she is called more often. She serves as a feminine expression of the Divine, offering prosperity to those who follow her wise counsel. The more well-known female image in Proverbs, however, is found in chapter 31, the "godly wife and mother" much exalted in some traditional circles as the ideal of womanhood. Feminist scholars have often noted the narrative transition from powerful goddess in Proverbs 1–9 to godly wife in Proverbs 31 as a "domestication" of the feminine divine.[5] Over time, and through the lens of our secular culture, that image of womanhood has devolved into a distinctly Western image of femininity: think pearls, a floral sheath, brunch cooking on the stove, and a Donna Reed toothy smile for the camera. The Baptists down the road from me *love* that verse. They put it up on their changeable letter sign every year on Mother's Day. There's nothing inherently wrong with that image of womanhood. But to call it "ideal" implies that other expressions of the feminine are somehow subpar and not desirable to God.

In her book, *Jesus Feminist,* Sara Bessey also points out how many of these traditional notions of ideal Christian womanhood are distinctly Western, privileged perspectives that simply will not fly in much of the world. She says, "If [biblical womanhood] can't be enjoyed by a woman in Haiti, or even by the woman hailed in Scripture, the same way it can by a middle-class woman in Canada, then biblical womanhood must be more than this."[6]

The term "more than this" is key to understanding gender and identity from a progressive angle. It is not that we want to reject, out of hand, all traditional expressions of masculine and feminine identity—this much is implied when fundamentalists accuse all feminists of being man-haters. There is nothing inherently wrong with being a girly-girl, or a manly-man, if that is who you are. What *is* deeply problematic is the assumption that these rigid binaries are the only acceptable way to be, and that being anything "other" is to somehow be less than. On the contrary, God calls us to be *more than.* To be more than just male or female, to be more than the world's image or expectation of us, to be more than the bodies in which we live. The holiness within us is complex and multi-layered—far more than how we dress, how we move in our bodies, or even who we love. Once we can embrace the complexity of the created self, we can better understand the nature of God, and better accept the diversity present at the table of God's blessing.

In the New Testament, there are no shortage of female role models for ministry and leadership: Mary and Martha, and their active presence among Jesus and the disciples; the women who stayed at the cross through the long, dark hours of his suffering, long after the men had left in fear, or helplessness; and Lydia, who clearly evangelized her whole dang town. We could go on.

But for so many, the long list of called and gifted women do not stand up in the face of a few errant verses, calling for the silence of women. Namely those proof-text verses that appear in 1 Corinthians and 1 Timothy. I know them by heart, because they've been slung at me my whole life by friends, strangers, and Internet trolls. But, as Jimmy Carter and countless biblical scholars have pointed out, those verses were intended for a particular purpose, a particular place and time. But the narrative stories of women who lead can reach across those boundaries of time and space, teaching us what women can do, when empowered; and what the Church can do, in fullness of life, when it lets go of those archaic boundaries that are rooted in antiquity.

Interesting that Paul, who was known to have "silenced" women (if that's what he meant to do, which is debatable) is the same one who said, so boldly, "There is no longer Jew or Greek, there is no longer slave or free, there is no longer *male and female; for all of you are one in Christ Jesus*" (Gal. 3:28, italics added). Not to be accused of proof-texting, I should qualify that Paul was speaking particularly to divisions between Jews and Gentiles in the early Christian community. But Paul's inclusion of men *and* women there is significant, especially considering the other times when the omission of women's gifts seems glaring.

Their sons *and* their daughters will prophesy. May it be so.

AROUND THE TABLE:
QUESTIONS FOR DISCUSSION

1. In what ways can we reinforce equality in the home, regardless of family makeup or the gender roles expressed in our own household?

2. What kinds of language, slurs, or assumptions about gender and sexuality do you find especially troubling in your social circles, workplace, or faith community?
3. Why is it important for youth and children to see both men and women leading and speaking in church, as well as other areas of community life?
4. How can the faith community move further toward understanding full and sacred embodiment, beyond gender or sexual identity?

10
Authenticity: Being Who You Are

In the course of dreaming up this book, I've had conversations with different groups of people about values. Leadership retreats, women's retreats, clergy retreats, church groups of various ages and life stations, friends and family, and online with blog readers and other writers. I wouldn't call it formal research, by any stretch, but it's been a valuable process for thinking about what matters most to us, and how we let ourselves and our relationships be shaped by that which gives the greatest meaning.

Every conversation has been helpful, but I remember one moment, in particular, when a light came on for me. It was a fairly informal gathering at church, of mostly older people— mostly older women, in fact, with maybe a few men. We were discussing the values that we picked up as children, both for better and for worse.

Most people could think of ways they had learned honesty, hard work, loyalty, and kindness—things like that. But I started noticing a trend: that most people had also picked up, somewhere along the way, the need *to hide something*. For some, it was that Mom and Dad weren't happy at home. For others, maybe it had to do with money (scarcity) and projecting an image contrary to reality. Putting on a good face no matter what was troubling them. Some felt the need to cover for a family member with a mental illness, or a drinking problem. It was like that, for nearly everyone, when they were just children.

"So what I'm hearing, is that you never learned to be authentic," I said. "Or, that, instead, you learned the value of . . . well, what's the opposite of authenticity?"

There were crickets for a moment. Though nearly everyone could think of a time or a situation in which they'd been expected to project an image other than that of their reality, we all struggled to articulate the "value" that had actually rushed in to fill this particular void.

So we're all thinking, *what is the opposite of authenticity?* And just as I'm waiting for somebody to say, "Let's ask Siri," the lone man in the room spoke up.

"Pretense," he said simply. And a hush fell over the room.

Dang, that was *deep.*

The man who answered is retired clergy. I'd imagine clergy of that generation witnessed their share of pretense. So when he said that, it was a major lightbulb moment: the realization that, sometimes, even the absence of a certain value is, in itself, a value. In other words—not all values are desirable ones. And kids sometimes pick up stuff that we don't know we're putting out there.

It was a sobering thought. And maybe it wasn't the big lightbulb moment for everyone that it was for me, but it did reveal one of the fundamental ways that traditional family values can fail, for all the best intentions of the parents and faith leaders who teach them. Those traditional values, for all the good they can do, often value pretense above all else: *Don't tell anyone you're on antidepressants. Everything's fine at home. Oh, they're just roommates.* And that kind of facade can be profoundly destructive—for children, for families, and for the churches in which we practice shared faith.

It is a fatal flaw of fundamentalism to value pretense over relationship: over and above the gay child who has finally mustered the courage to tell you; or perpetuating stigma around mental illness; or forcing a woman to stay in an abusive relationship; or keeping a struggling couple from getting the counseling that could save their marriage. On and on, in countless ways, the burdensome work of maintaining a facade can be deeply destructive.

It was in this moment that I realized that one of my deepest desires for my children is that they be fully who they are, knowing that, even in imperfection, they are deeply beloved children of God.

Of course, there is a place for discipline. There is a time for teaching healthy boundaries. And responsibility. And all sorts of other values that will help them navigate the world in responsible ways. But with that sense of love and belonging as a foundation, much of the rest falls into place. Children and youth who are *authenticated* by family and community aren't as likely to retreat when they're in trouble or when they're in a difficult spot of discernment or transition.

The value of authentic living reaches far beyond parenting too. Marriages are happier and more fulfilling when both partners are able to be who they are.

Communities that welcome and affirm people—meeting them where they are rather than meeting them at the door with a long list of expected beliefs and behaviors—those communities are more diverse, a *heck* of a lot more fun, and, ultimately, more life-giving to community and world.

A big part of being who we are is letting ourselves be fully *where* we are. Showing up, present moment, at home in the world.

I was not the mom sobbing into my latte. Nor was I the mom skipping and cheering down the hall because it was my first moment of freedom in five years. No, on my kid's first day of kindergarten, I was the mom frantically stashing school supplies into the cubby, because I hadn't thought to bring them on meet-the-teacher night. I was the mom noticing that I was suddenly the only parent still in the room, as the teacher started her welcome routine for the students.

We hadn't even been in town a year yet, at that point, and were still in a rental house. I knew that we would be buying a house again, maybe soon. In a town that has a school in nearly every neighborhood, even a move within a mile of our house would put us in a different elementary zone. That meant we started the first day of school knowing we might be at a different school by Christmas. It was a little dizzying to think of all the school preparations and excitement we'd gone through, and all the work teachers do to make kids feel at home and settled, just to uproot again.

Rewind about 30 years, to my first day of kindergarten. On my way to school, I met a kid named Jason. We met on the school bus, just like Forrest Gump and Jenny. And living in a semirural area as we did at that time, the ride to school was a pretty long haul. At least, it seemed long to my 5-year-old self. So somewhere between my house and Johnson Elementary, I found my first friend. We were neighbors, as it turned out, and we wound up in the same class every year until sixth grade. We still had many classes together through high school, including a performance choir that traveled. I took him his homework when he was sick. He came (under duress) to my dance recitals. We often carpooled when we were older and driving. We prescreened each other's love interests. And while we didn't always heed each other's advice, we always later wished we had. We went to colleges that were 15 minutes apart. We spent more time together in some years, less in others; but he was with me every moment of a very difficult summer, when there was a scary guy in the picture. And we wound up living in the same apartment complex—completely by chance—in our 20s.

Which is to say, I walked away from my daughter's first day of school hoping that she would meet her Forrest but also kind of hoping that she wouldn't. I didn't think my heart could take her coming home with stories of new best friends and favorite teachers, knowing that we might only be at this school for a little while. I felt the impulse to guard her from attachment; from connections too meaningful or a place that felt too right.

And then I realized that I was really hoping for her not to love too much. That I was encouraging her, right out of the gate on her first day of formal education, to put up boundaries that would prevent her from getting too close to anyone. In a subtle way, I was setting her up to avoid vulnerability by guarding her heart at all times. In essence, that is the same thing as asking someone to not be fully themselves. Was I guilty of teaching the value of pretense?

First day of school or otherwise, I never want to be the mom who tells my kids not to love too much. I never want them to be afraid of being who they are.

With the world coming unglued in the myriad ways it seems to be these days, *it is not possible to love too much*. Who am I to say that we shouldn't feel connected to someone who's only in our lives for a short while? Whether it's for ten weeks or ten minutes? If I am a person of faith—and I sure like to think that I am—I believe that any measure of love can move in some way to transform the world.

Isn't that what all this Jesus stuff adds up to?

We cannot love too much. We can't be too accepting, too forgiving, too "politically correct," or too risky with our welcome.

And anyway, we don't get to know, when we meet someone, what our long-term relationship will amount to. We can't anticipate how much we can trust or be real or allow our hearts to be broken. If we could know, then love would be easy and safe. And if love were easy and safe, it would not bear nearly the transformative potential that it does.

I didn't *know* that my first friend in kindergarten was going to be *that* friend. That he would be such a big part of my life for so long. I didn't know, when I first met the girl three dorm rooms down from me, that I would be adopted into her family; that we would travel together and be in each other's weddings, and that I would drive a great distance to be with her when her father died.

When my brother was an annoying 8-year-old, wanting to hang out with me and my "cool" friends (we weren't that cool), I would never have imagined that there would come a day when I would call him to talk. *On purpose.*

I didn't know, on my first date with my husband, that we would travel the world, move across the country a few times, and have two kids (and a dog) together somewhere along the way.

And when we first bring children into the world, we can't know who they're going to be. We can't know how they will dazzle or disappoint us; what struggles they will face, what brand of extraordinary they will be, or how their hearts will break. But my, how we love them anyway. Isn't that the point?

Loving anyway opens the door for miraculous lifelong connections or even connections that might be for a particular season, but still shape us in some significant way. How would we ever find our people if we did not—for at least a few critical moments in life—love with the abandon of a child?

Every day, we send our kids out into the world, knowing that the reckless way in which they love makes them vulnerable to heartbreak. We can teach them to fear that—to live and love with caution and only ever make shallow connections to the world around them—or we can send them out believing that *ten minutes on the bus can change your life. And maybe the world.*

Of course, we also teach them safe boundaries; make sure they are surrounded with trusted adults until they learn how to filter their interactions in safe ways. But ultimately, we aim to do that in a way that doesn't make them afraid of the world, in a way that doesn't make them draw inward and live small.

Vulnerability guru Brené Brown has this to say about authentic living:

> Authenticity is the daily practice of letting go of who we think we're supposed to be and embracing who we are. Choosing authenticity means: cultivating the courage to be imperfect, to set boundaries, and to allow ourselves to be vulnerable; exercising the compassionate that comes from knowing that we are all made of strength and struggle; and

nurturing the connection and sense of belonging that can only happen when we believe that we are enough. . . .

Sacrificing who we are for the sake of what other people think just isn't worth it. Yes, there can be authenticity growing pains for the people around us, but in the end, being true to ourselves is the best gift we can give to the people we love. When I let go of trying to be everything to everyone, I had much more time, attention, love, and connection with important people in my life.

Dig deep. Get Deliberate: Whenever I am faced with a vulnerable situation, I get deliberate with my intentions by repeating this to myself: "Don't shrink. Don't puff up. Stand on your sacred ground."[1]

Showing up every day—being who we are, and rooting ourselves in the present—is sacred ground. It is a holy territory that we don't always realize we're standing on until some person or circumstance begins to slide it out from under us. The work of claiming that territory is hard work. Sometimes it takes an extraordinary measure of mindfulness and spiritual discipline to keep ourselves grounded in that way of openness and connection. This has always been true. But that work of authenticity has become even more difficult in the age of social media.

Naming our values and learning who we are in a sea of our peers is a critical part of the coming-of-age process. Children of a certain age learn to process that which they have absorbed at home and in the faith community, through the lens of friends their age and with increasing amounts of freedom to wander beyond the boundaries of the safety net. They try on different personas—some combination of Mom and/or Dad (whether they like it or not), whatever pop star is "it" today, and whatever book or movie character most embodies an antithesis to the expected norm from the family. It can be a subtle rebellion or a dramatic one, but it all comes down to that one critical question: *Who am I when I'm not with my family?*

PRACTICING AUTHENTICITY AT HOME

Of course, being who we are away from home begins with what we learn at home.

In the digital age, this fundamental question of development has been dramatically complicated by Instagram, Snapchat, Facebook, Twitter, and whatever new thing will evolve between the time of my writing this and your reading of it. The exercise of cultivating an online presence is almost a given part of growing up now. The temptation that comes with that territory—the impulse to create a profile based on a completely false self, compiled of celebrity gossip, Pinterest images, and friends' expectations—is not just an illness for the young. Adults of all ages fall victim to the selfie culture that demands we be always "on," always edited for flaws, and always connected (without really being connected). It reaches into every demographic these days. However, children and youth are especially vulnerable as they balance this new and greatly uncharted media territory with the age-old work of becoming.

Today's parents—Gen Xers and, to a certain extent, older Millennials—are the first generation of parents to have to navigate this minefield with their children. Which is an unsettling prospect, considering we are all just figuring it out ourselves.

To suggest shielding our kids from this element of culture is like thinking we can keep them from breathing the polluted air. Media is that much a part of life now. We might limit screen time, police passwords, and withhold devices until an appropriate age. These are all good practices, but they will not utterly sequester our children from the media culture that saturates everything.

What we can do—what I hope we are doing—is to give them the tools to process the world and their sense of self in healthy ways. Ways that will transcend their desire to project a certain image and that will keep them connected IRL (#inreallife).

The first step is to let them see us being real, and that they see us looking them in the eye without our phone or i-whatever in hand (says the mom who has spent her summer at the laptop, furiously typing towards a book deadline). There is a great deal of really precious shaming out there these days: "I *never* let my kids see me working at a computer," and "*Always* turn your phone off when the family is in the room," and "Stop taking pictures and be in the moment!" There is some measure of truth to these sentiments, but be wary of anything that includes the word "always" or "never."

That said: it is good practice, and just good manners, to put down the phone when the kids are talking to us. To turn down the car radio when they are asking us something. To not take the work call in the middle of family dinner. To not always have a television on in the background so that real conversation is punctuated with commercials, gun violence, and other people's stuff.

These small but intentional practices, over time, add up to kids knowing how to be *where they are*. And this will help them to remember, ultimately, *who* they are—and to whom they belong.

My friend Kara is a minister, as was her mother, with whom I once had the privilege to go on a mission trip to Africa. Ann, like Kara, was nearly six feet tall, blonde, and a powerful force of love and compassion. I watched her sit at the bedside of AIDS patients and sing hymns through tears. I also saw her fiercely advocate for sex education and access to protection for people who had been given a great deal of misinformation about how this disease was spread. I was with her on a trip that she took at great risk to her personal health—forgoing chemotherapy for a recently reappeared cancer until after our travel—because this was a lifelong dream of hers, and she was committed to seeing it through.

Ann passed away about six months after that trip, and I have always been grateful for those glimpses of her strong witness to the power of being present. But I feel like I get more than glimpses in knowing Kara, seeing the ways in which her ministry, and who she is as a mother, are shaped by that same love, faith, and fearlessness.

Kara tells the story of how, when she and her brothers were growing up, they would leave the house on a Friday night. Other parents would say, "Don't do anything stupid" or "You'll be in big trouble if . . ." or any number of specific instructions for behaving themselves. But Ann always said the same thing: "*Remember who you are.*"

Clearly, that loaded instruction hit the mark, if her adult children now remember it all these years later. "Remember who you are." Imagine if that single statement was all we needed to send our kids out, safely and strongly into the world. Imagine that we did such an effective job of rooting all these other values that a simple "remember who you are" every now and then was all they needed to call that good news up to the surface.

That's the best we can hope for. That's what all the rest of this is for.

One of the best ways to cultivate a life of authenticity is to create a safe space in our homes for people to be themselves. Sometimes that is messy and uncomfortable, but for the health of our children—and for all of our relationships—it is the best work we can do.

One way to do this is to value and model truth-telling. That means not reacting to kids' uncomfortable questions with horror. They will ask about sex; they will ask about violence they see on the news; they will ask about the completely age-inappropriate thing that they heard from their friend's older sibling; they will want to know why you and your spouse or you and your mother are fighting. They want to know *all the things* because kids are one big giant walking question mark. Sometimes practicing good boundaries means that we can't give them all the information. But we can engage them in honest and forthright ways that don't shame the question, and that build a foundation for open communication that can evolve along with them.

That means being present to an anxiety, concern, or interest, even if they aren't ready to bear the full weight of the knowledge yet. To hear questions without brushing them aside or reacting negatively to their curiosity, while also avoiding a "Don't worry, be happy" kind of response. Brushing aside a genuine concern or glossing over doubt makes for some of the biggest pretense-teaching moments. If kids have big questions to which we don't know the answer, we can wonder with them. If they are worried about something, we can do our best to soothe the anxious spirit, and then we can be with them in the uncertainty. If they want to know about big-people things—sex and war are the big ones that immediately come to mind, though there are plenty of others—then we give them an abridged version that begins an open discussion, understanding that these things are ongoing conversations we don't always have to completely "answer" or "fix" in the moment. In the meantime, we are fully present with them in the space between.

We can also affirm the gifts that we see in our children—and not just the most visible and performance-based ones. For instance, we praise kids for good grades, excelling in sports or the arts, or winning the science fair or an essay contest. These are certainly moments to be celebrated. But we can also dig a little deeper, and articulate for our children the more fundamental sparks that we see in them—those things that will outlast an injury that takes them out of sports, and will sustain them through a rough patch in algebra.

If we praise a child for being generous, for being kind, for being responsible; if we note the way they reach out to a new kid who's feeling lonely, or help around the house without being asked, or keep trying when something is challenging; these character traits, already a part of who they are, will inform the roots of their identity. These traits will rise to the surface under pressure, or in times of disappointment (because you can't win the science fair every time), and through the tenuous wilderness of adolescent bullying.

If the groundwork of "who we are" is laid, not with achievement and merit-based praise, but with embodied values and our core belovedness as children of God, concerns about image and the burden of pretense become miraculously diminished in the face of learning how to be a whole person from a young age.

Let the weird kid be weird. Let the vegetarian kid do her thing. Let the musician in a family of football players march to his drum. But more importantly, if we let the language of acceptance drown out the mantra of "what will the neighbors think," then we hold the power to transform the world—for our children, and through them.

PRACTICING AUTHENTICITY IN COMMUNITY

The recent mass exodus from institutional religion shows that the Church's traditional teaching formula is losing its effectiveness among contemporary families. That model has been primarily instructional: teach what the Bible says about God, what to believe about God, and how to follow the rules reflected in that understanding of God.

Many pastors, sociologists, historians, theologians, and two-bit bloggers (me) from all sorts of contexts have made their guesses—educated and otherwise—about what is causing a growing number of people to reject this approach to faith. The fundamentalists will say that we've made it too easy and tried to be all things to all people. Progressives say that the Church has long been too judgmental and hypocritical, and we are now reaping what's been sown for centuries. Some say that worship is too dull, while others say we've tried too hard to make it entertaining.

There is probably some measure of truth to each of these assertions. But at the heart of the mass exodus of the past few decades of American faith lies the corporate sin of pretense: religious organizations have historically valued the appearance of faith above all else; "right belief" often takes precedence over right relationships with neighbors; complex social issues have been met with black-and-white, right-and-wrong answers; and doubt has often been met with swift and certain rejection.

Ultimately, more and more people find that there is no place for doubt and uncertainty within the faith, which leads them to suspect that there is no room for *them* in the faith. No room for their questions, and no room for who they are. And so, they leave. With the digital age, the readiness of worldwide news around the clock and all the knowledge of creation at our fingertips, many parts of family life and culture have evolved rapidly over the past few decades. In many ways, the Church has evolved too. In other ways—or rather, in certain contexts and settings—the Church has just doubled down on its insistence that believers adhere to a particular expression of the faith. Clearly, that kind of rigid doctrine works in some places. But in others, it puts people in the painful all-or-nothing position of having to either pretend things they don't really believe are true or having to abandon the faith and community that might still, in many ways, be meaningful to them.

Whether intentionally or not, the institutional church teaches pretense when it demands absolute adherence to human-made legalisms.

But through the spiritual practice of authenticity, we can create space within our communities for doubt. We can encourage children's questions, however heretical they might be. We can learn to meet people where they are, engaging difficult questions, learning to be comfortable in places of uncertainty, and admitting, together, that we don't have all the answers. Faith is found in the in-between places anyway. Those places where we don't know it all, if we can bear to admit as much, are most often where God can move through and do a new thing.

It is time—it is so far past time—that the Church begins to tear down the walls it has built up between itself and the world, and between its people and their neighbors. It is time to dwell less in absolutes, and more in holy maybes.

The community that can truly value authentic community over right belief may begin to discover a greater bandwidth for mission. When doubts and questions are welcomed as gifts for ministry, there are far more people at the table to carry the weight of ministry.

Beyond just accepting the questions of children, and the doubts of most grown-ups, the work of sharing authentic faith in community extends to how we welcome those who've long been deemed "unacceptable" by the gospel of pretense.

The Church lives authentic compassion when it rejects the stigma of mental illness.

The Church lives authentic welcome when it welcomes the LGBTQ population, long excluded by some oversimplified proof-texting of a scant few verses of Scripture.

The Church embodies authentic witness when it can embrace the single parent, the newly divorced, and the same-sex couple, all in the same breath.

The Church models authentic faith when it meets the stranger, the immigrant, the refugee, the one from the edges, in a posture of deepest humility.

This way of being God's people—the way that values doubt and uncertainty and the space for the mysteries of becoming— is not always popular. In many circles, it is deemed sinful, false, taking the "easy" way, and any other number of things that imply we have abandoned our true calling to live the gospel.

But actually, the Church answers authentic calling when it abandons the facade of having all the answers, and engages deeply the difficult questions of our time. When it places the health of neighbor above the authority of institution. And when its people recognize that, perhaps, within their own open uncertainty is the space where God might do a new thing. The space where love of neighbor can transcend attachment to creed.

AUTHENTICITY IN SCRIPTURE

O Lord, you have searched me and known me.
You know when I sit down and when I rise up;
    you discern my thoughts from far away.
You search out my path and my lying down,
    and are acquainted with all my ways.
Even before a word is on my tongue,

O Lord, you know it completely.
You hem me in, behind and before,
　and lay your hand upon me.
Such knowledge is too wonderful for me;
　it is so high that I cannot attain it.
Where can I go from your spirit?
　Or where can I flee from your presence?
If I ascend to heaven, you are there;
　if I make my bed in Sheol, you are there.
If I take the wings of the morning
　and settle at the farthest limits of the sea,
even there your hand shall lead me,
　and your right hand shall hold me fast.
If I say, "Surely the darkness shall cover me,
　and the light around me become night,"
even the darkness is not dark to you;
　the night is as bright as the day,
　for darkness is as light to you.
For it was you who formed my inward parts;
　you knit me together in my mother's womb.
I praise you, for I am fearfully and wonderfully made.
　Wonderful are your works;
that I know very well.
　My frame was not hidden from you,
when I was being made in secret,
　intricately woven in the depths of the earth.
Your eyes beheld my unformed substance.
In your book were written
　all the days that were formed for me,
　when none of them as yet existed.
How weighty to me are your thoughts, O God!
　How vast is the sum of them!
I try to count them—they are more than the sand;
　I come to the end—I am still with you.
. . . .
Search me, O God, and know my heart;
　test me and know my thoughts.
See if there is any wicked way in me,
　and lead me in the way everlasting.

Psalm 139

God formed us in the womb. God looks at us, all "fearfully, wonderfully made," and calls us good. In that blessing is an invitation to live fully and generously, allowing ourselves to be shaped in the love that formed us. Fearfully and wonderfully.

That same invitation unfolds throughout all of Scripture: in the roots of Eden (Genesis again); in the traveling mercies that bound the people of God together in the desert; in those days when the disciples drew close to Jesus, gathered around a table like the village of one's own choosing; and in the resurrection moments that reached so far beyond the empty tomb, and into the days of the early Church.

Those are all important chapters in the story of who we are—and who God is to us. But there's just something about a psalm. There's something about a psalm that can capture all that existential and theological stuff, but deliver it with a healthy dose of art, poetry, and song. There's something about a psalm that works at the bedside of a dying loved one in a way that no other Scripture can serve. There's something about a psalm that calls us into celebratory worship in a way that no repetitive praise chorus can quite capture.

When nothing else can quite articulate the joy, the anguish, the complete mystery of being human—then there's probably a psalm for that.

Poetry and song are the language of the spirit. That truth reaches beyond words on the pages of Scripture and into our everyday lives: a gift by which we process relationships, experiences, and the world around us.

Brittany Howard, of Alabama Shakes fame, gave an interview in which she talked about her life growing up in a small town. Her family owned and ran a junkyard in Athens, Alabama, and their home sat in the midst of it. They lived in a literal trash heap where other people came to leave the castoffs of their too-full lives. To some, that would sound like the most miserable kind of existence. But look how she talks about it:

> We lived down a long gravel driveway, and you're driving
> through these woods and then you cross a bridge over a

creek. And then you keep going up this hill, and on either side of you it just starts filling in with junk cars, newer cars, boats, motorcycles, a shop. It's all around you. And then you get to the top of the hill and that's where, um . . . we grew up in a little trailer, but it was really nice.

My mom was really good at making our home—no matter what our situation was—always felt like a home, always felt really nice. And I played with our animals. We had a lot of different kinds of animals. I grew up on a farm in a sense, but it was always a junkyard. So it was a really interesting way to grow up, because I would be playing on all of these stacked-up cars, which is super-dangerous, but then I'd also go run around the woods with my dog, and go play in the creek. . . . The way I think of it is, you're surrounded by the junkyard. Think of it like a hurricane, and you're in the eye of it. The little patch of grass that has the animals and the little trailer and then the rest was, to me, was like a labyrinth. It was an amusement park.[2]

There is no scarcity here. There is only beauty, with an edge of reality, in this loving description of a childhood home. The rest of Howard's life was not all "amusement park." Her sister lost her vision, and later died at age thirteen of retinal cancer. Her parents split up, then she and her mother moved to another town. But as she tells her story, the listener can plainly hear how that green, lovely place in "the eye of the hurricane" remained a grounding force in her life, and gave life to the Grammy-winning artistic genius whom we witness today.

Authenticity is the art of finding the beauty of what *is*, not what we hope we should be or what someone else thinks we should be. When we are rooted in family and given a strong sense of belonging, that authentic life takes root around us—in every stage of life and regardless of changing circumstances. We can be truly who we are, knowing that "who we are" is a blessed and beloved child of God.

In Scripture, we see how the words of poetry and song—in the Psalms and elsewhere—become more than words, taking on a life of their own. In the same way, the origin narratives, the stories of Israel in the wilderness, and the Gospel texts become a sacred core of meaning. These stories give life to our life, draw us back to a place of connectedness when we have been wandering, and send us out again, secure in knowing—and remembering—who we are.

Authentic life is a rich life of the spirit. We find that richness in art and poetry and music; in the sacred stories of faith that have been given to our care; and in the family connections that, if we are lucky, are ours from birth. Having been given such a gift, it is the most natural thing in the world that we learn to make more room at the table. We learn to open doors and windows, build bridges, make more bread, pour more wine, tell better stories, and draw a much wider circle around our understanding of "neighbor." We are safe and beloved at the heart of that circle—a green, growing thing of beauty—whatever else may pile up around us.

AROUND THE TABLE:
QUESTIONS FOR DISCUSSION

1. Did you ever learn the value of pretense as a child? And have you come to value authenticity as an adult?
2. What are some of the ways that secular culture values pretense over authenticity?
3. Can you name some people in Scripture who struggled with the tension between these two values?
4. How does your faith community empower individuals and families to live authentic lives?

Conclusion

Some elements of this book will invite a visceral, negative reaction from certain corners of the faith community. Welcoming LGBTQ folks to the table; questioning of a "literal" reading of Scripture; and even challenging certain elements of the secular American-Christian narrative: this is all it takes to be written off as a radical leftist hippie, in the current social-political climate. "Not a real Christian," some will say (and have said). "These are not *my* family values!" others will shout. I can already hear the echoes of "liberal agenda" as we speak.

But what could be more Christian than seeking to live a life that mirrors the compassionate, nonviolent, and inclusive way of Jesus? What could be more family-centered than shaping a world that *values* all human life in its many expressions? How could we claim to value abundant life without protecting the earth from the ill effects of capitalism and a fear-based narrative of scarcity?

Some days, I have laughed out loud at myself for thinking I could write about family values. I, who fight with my husband about . . . what was it again? We already forgot. I, who have been known to induce a full-on meltdown in my kids because they forgot (again) to flush the toilet. I, who moved half the country away from my parents, grandparents, brother, and all my in-laws and only see them once or twice a year. I, who so clearly, still have so much to figure out.

I've also found it laughable that I might somehow have a voice that qualifies as any kind of "progressive," which is how I nuanced this conversation. In spite of my feminist, left-leaning ways, my day-to-day life is about as traditional as one can be. I live in the suburbs with my husband, to whom I have been married for 13 years; we have both been married only to each other. We have a girl-child, a boy-child, and a dog. A full-time job. Two cars. An apple tree in our fenced-in yard.

I'm grateful for every bit of it. But I also realize how privileged I am: the economic privilege that led to my education, which led to secure employment; the white privilege that means no one ever looks at me funny when I walk down the suburban streets at night; the straight, cisgender privilege that means my marriage is blessed by the religious institution and sanctioned by the government, and I've never had to fight for any of my rights.

As much as I have learned from my mistakes as an imperfect wife, mother, and human being, I have learned just as much from my privilege. Or rather, from the practice of noting my privilege. I view the convergence of these two realities—my own significant shortcomings, and the simultaneous unfair advantages that life has granted me—as an invitation, pure and simple. It's an invitation to walk daily with gratitude; to root my children in the kind of love and belonging that will empower them to do good in the world; and to uproot some of those unjust systems that tip so many favors in my direction, at the expense of others. This awareness is what sets an emerging, progressive values system apart from the traditional, "one man and one woman" kind of values. The latter is rooted in demands: expectations that one person's family should look exactly like the next; and a denial of the whole personhood of those who don't conform to the mold. Those values, though well-intentioned and right for some families, can be deeply harmful when reduced to a sound bite and enforced as a one-size-fits-all standard of family life.

Moving beyond that singular expectation and breathing life into the family that "is" opens up some creative space for the art of making our lives together. Lives that move and live and sing and transform, beyond just the telling. There is no one way to be a family, and that is the best news of all. We are all invited to that shared work of loving our people, building our village, and righting the tilted world. No matter how we vote, what we believe, or who we love—this is our gift and our calling.

For all the progress over the last generation or so, voices of hatred toward minorities, women, immigrants, and LGBT people seem to be getting stronger and louder. That those voices often come from certain corners of our own government is no consolation. If anything, the most recent election cycle nudged us backward—or, rather, turned us inward. Much is uncertain, but whatever the coming seasons hold, we know this for certain: voices of compassion, nonviolence, and justice are more important now than ever. Our best hope is to equip our children with a language of love that is more than sound bites, more than words. Maybe the most radically transformative thing we can do for the world is to raise compassionate, peace-loving children.

There is a highway in the desert. I'm pretty sure that is either Scripture or a Neil Young song, possibly both—but there is a highway in the desert that connects six of our most spectacular National Parks. Stretching from the Arizona-Mexico border to the Montana-Canada border, Highway 89 runs by the Grand Canyon, Zion, Bryce, Yellowstone, the Grand Tetons, and Glacier. From the desert chasms to the icy peaks and all the mountain drama in between, it is 1,800 miles of pure amazement. And when we were young and childless and free, my husband and I did the whole dang thing. In a Toyota Camry, with a tent in the car. And a Marriott Employee Discount card in our back pockets, just for good luck.

We took this trip during a transitional season, as we were moving from Kentucky—where we were both born and raised and had lived all our lives—to Arizona, where I'd accepted a call to my first pastorate. To say we had no idea what we were doing would be an understatement of Teton proportion. We were 20-something, basically newlywed, and leaving the mother country for the first time. So it should surprise no one that we had a flat tire in Utah; a fried battery in Idaho; a broken rearview mirror in Montana; and something else that happened around Wyoming that, clearly, I've blocked out.

But it was an amazing adventure, even though we were broke. It was an amazing adventure, even though we were technically, as one of my horrified friends pointed out, "basically homeless!" And all along the way, every time something broke, somebody turned up to help us fix it. Like the guys who had to take a sledge hammer to get our flat tire off the car, because the rim was bent; or the many gracious souls who offered directions to some lost kids, long before anyone had ever heard of Siri or a Garmin.

The Phoenix housing market disaster lay in our future, unseen. As did a job where, I would quickly realize, I'd be in way over my head. As did a pregnancy with a difficult bedrest, plus other unknown quantities that would challenge, stretch, and even pain us.

But also ahead of us: two amazing little people who would be piled in the backseat, books and stuffed animal pets and all, by the time we moved again; a village, the first of many, that would support and sustain us; and a family of faith that would be first my exodus and then my Eden, by the time it was all said and done.

Somewhere on that long stretch of road, in all that diverse terrain, I learned an important truth that would serve me in all that lay ahead. In becoming a wife and mother, in leading a dying church to live again, and in all the times of transition since; I always think of those Highway 89 days and remember that even in the desert, you're never alone.

It's like that. The landscape changes from desert to mountain to desert again; we never know where we're going, or what joy and hardship are waiting up around that next curve. But we keep moving anyway, assembling the rag-tag assortment of people we collect and gather along the way. This is the nature of family. We live together at the convergence of our own imperfections, and all the ways we can make each other better by just living together and being who we are. Our great hope is that we can change the terrain as we go, and, someday, be the roadside assistance that someone else is waiting for.

Notes

Chapter 1: Compassion

1. Annie Kratzsch, "This Rare Moment," This Rare Day (blog), August 18, 2015, http://www.thisrareday.com/blog/2015/8/18/this-rare -moment.
2. http://kindcraft.org/our-story.

Chapter 2: Abundance

1. Lynne Twist, *The Soul of Money* (New York: Norton, 2003), 43–44.
2. Elizabeth Cline, "Where Does Discarded Clothing Go?" *The Atlantic,* July 18, 2014, http://www.theatlantic.com/business /archive/2014/07/where-does-discarded-clothing-go/374613.
3. More resources at http://centerforfaithandgiving.org/Resources /tabid/755/Default.aspx.
4. Walter Brueggemann, "The Liturgy of Abundance, the Myth of Scarcity," *The Christian Century*, March 24, 1999, http://www.christian century.org/article/2012-01/liturgy-abundance-myth-scarcity.

Chapter 3: Sabbath

1. Sonja M. Stewart and Jerome Berryman, *Young Children and Worship* (Louisville, KY: Westminster/John Knox Press, 1989).
2. Jordi Lippe-McGraw, "Americans Squandered 658 Million Vacation Days Last Year," *Travel and Leisure*, June 15, 2016, http:// www.travelandleisure.com/travel-tips/travel-trends/americans-unused -vacation-days.
3. According to statistics from the Economic Policy Institute, see Elise Gould, "Millions of Working People Don't Get Paid Time Off for Holidays or Vacation," September 1, 2015, http://www.epi.org

/publication/millions-of-working-people-dont-get-paid-time-off-for
-holidays-or-vacation/.

4. Wendell Berry, "Two Economies," in *Home Economics* (Berkeley: Counterpoint, 1987), 54–75.

5. Barbara Brown Taylor, *An Altar in the World* (New York: Harper One, 2009), 121.

Chapter 4: Nonviolence

1. Joel B. Green and Mark D. Baker, *Recovering the Scandal of the Cross: Atonement in New Testament and Contemporary Contexts* (Downers Grove, IL: InterVarsity Press, 2000), 90.

2. Green and Baker, *Recovering the Scandal*, 15.

3. Walter Wink, "Jesus and Nonviolence: A Third Way," in Michael G. Long, ed., *Christian Peace and Nonviolence: A Documentary History* (Maryknoll: Orbis Books, 2011).

4. "A Victim Treats His Mugger Right," *StoryCorps*, produced by Michael Garofalo, *Morning Edition*, NPR, March 28, 2008, http:// www.npr.org/templates/transcript/transcript.php?storyId=89164759.

5. "Elementary School Clerk Says She Convinced Suspect to Put His Weapons Down and Surrender," interview by Diane Sawyer, *World News with Diane Sawyer*, ABC News, August 20, 2013, Diane Sawyer, Mike Levine, Steve Osunsami, and Michael S. James, contributors, http://abcnews.go.com/US/elementary-school-clerk-convinced-suspect -put-weapons-surrender/story?id=20014879.

Chapter 5: Joy

1. "In Paducah, Artists Create Something from Nothing," by Noah Adams, *Morning Edition*, NPR, August 9, 2013, http://www .npr.org/2013/08/09/210130790/in-paducah-artists-create-something -from-nothing.

Chapter 7: Community

1. Andrew Palmer, "Clay County MO Resident Serves S'mores to Neighbors for 71 Days Straight," *Northland News*, Liberty, MO, September 2, 2015.

2. "A German Town in Decline Sees Refugees as Path to Revival," by Esme Nicholson, *Morning Edition*, NPR, September 3, 2015.

Chapter 8: Forgiveness

1. Donald B. Kraybill, Steven M. Nolt, and David L. Weaver-Zercher, *Amish Grace: How Forgiveness Transcended Tragedy* (San Francisco: Jossey-Bass, 2010), 192.
2. David Von Drehle, "How Do You Forgive a Murder?" *TIME*, November 2015.

Chapter 9: Equality

1. Jimmy Carter, "Losing My Religion for Equality," *The Age*, July 15, 2009, http://www.theage.com.au/federal-politics/losing-my-religion-for-equality-20090714-dk0v.html?stb=fb.
2. "Facts about Suicide," The Trevor Project, http://www.thetrevorproject.org/pages/facts-about-suicide.
3. Bill Moyers, "In God's Image," *Genesis: A Living Conversation*, PBS, October 22, 1996.
4. Jennifer Bird, *Permission Granted: Take the Bible into Your Own Hands* (Louisville, KY: Westminster John Knox Press, 2015), 18–19.
5. Claudia V. Camp, "Woman Wisdom: Bible," *Jewish Women: A Comprehensive Historical Encyclopedia*, March 1, 2009, Jewish Women's Archive, http://jwa.org/encyclopedia/article/woman-wisdom-bible.
6. Sarah Bessey, *Jesus Feminist: An Invitation to Revisit the Bible's View of Women* (New York: Howard Books, 2013), 100.

Chapter 10: Authenticity

1. Brené Brown, *The Gifts of Imperfection: Let Go of Who You Think You're Supposed to Be and Embrace Who You Are* (Center City, MN: Hazelden Publishing, 2010), 49–54.
2. "Alabama Shakes' Brittany Howard on Small Town Life, Big-Time Music," interviewed by Terry Gross, *Fresh Air*, NPR, January 28, 2016.

CPSIA information can be obtained
at www.ICGtesting.com
Printed in the USA
FSOW02n2014230317
32276FS